DECORATING

...the professional touch

DECORATING

...the professional touch

Carol Donayre Bugg, ASID, DDCD

Capital Lifestyles

CAPITAL
BOOKS, INC.

Capital Books, Inc.

Sterling, VA 20166

Also by Carol Donayre Bugg

Creating Great Guest Rooms

Divine Design

Smart & Simple Decorating

Dream Rooms for Real People

Capital Books, Inc.
P.O. Box 605
Herndon, Virginia 20172-0605

ISBN 978-1-933102-71-9

Library of Congress Cataloging-in-Publication Data
Bugg, Carol Donayre
 Decorating : the professional touch / Carol Donayre Bugg. -- 1st ed.
   p. cm.
 "Capital Lifestyles."
 Includes index.
 ISBN 978-1-933102-71-9 (alk. paper)
 1. Interior decoration. I. Title.

 NK2110.B82 2009
 747—dc22

                              2008051638
Printed in the United States of America on acid-free paper that meets the American National Standards Institute Z39-48 Standard.

First Edition

10 9 8 7 6 5 4 3 2

Dedication

For the two families that keep adding

zest to my life. . . the Buggs and

Decorating Den

Foreword   ix

Acknowledgments   xi

Introduction   What's A Decorator Got To Do with It?   xiii
                      12 reasons to hire an interior decorator

Chapter 1   My Decorating Odyssey   2
                      One decorator's path to a career in design

Chapter 2   The Decorating Den Story   18
                      The decorators who come to your home and listen to
                      your ideas

Chapter 6   Living Well Is All about Family
                      and Friends   68
                      Making everyday rooms warm and welcoming for
                      guests too

Chapter 7   Designing Windows   90
                      Why it's smart to leave the dressing of windows to
                      the pros

Chapter 8   The Charm of Color   106
                      Let the experts relieve your anxiety over color

Chapter 3   The Decorator's Decorator   30
                      Why it's so hard to decorate your own home

Chapter 4   Marrying His and Hers Personalities and
                      Possessions   38
                      Ways to combine the tastes of two strong individuals in
                      one room

Chapter 5   Decorating Is a Work in Progress   50
                      Debunking the myth that you have to start from scratch

Chapter 9   Art Appreciation   122
                      Using art to inspire a room's color scheme

Chapter 10   Evoking Quiet Elegance   138
                      Ways of making a serene haven of your home

Chapter 11   Personal Getaways for Women   150
                      Designing spaces to restore body and soul

Chapter 12   Everyone Needs a Great Desk   162
                      Selecting the right desk makes work a pleasure

Contents

Chapter 13   **Fostering Tradition**   172
Rooms with timeless appeal that never go out of style

Chapter 14   **The Allure of Glamour**   188
Ideas for creating luxurious atmospheres

Chapter 15   **Perpetuating a Key West Attitude**   198
Creating a year round paradise in your own home

Chapter 16   **Decorating a Home—One Room at a Time**   212
The pleasure of working with a decorator who cares

Epilogue   220

Photographer Credits   222

Decorator Credits   223

Foreword

*I*n my lifespan I have spent an inordinate amount of time explaining myself. This plight or delight, depending on the situation, began with my family name, Donayre. No one ever guesses its origin, Peruvian, nor manages without prodding to pronounce it correctly, *dough nigh ray*. At twenty-one I nearly escaped this exasperating challenge, but changed my mind before walking down the aisle to wed a boy with a simple surname. Instead, a decade later I chose to marry a gentleman with the short but provocative moniker of Bugg.

As for my chosen profession, the general public is unclear about the role of an interior decorator. I doubt if there are as many reports describing what a brain surgeon can do for you as there are articles attempting to explain what it is like to work with a decorator. I have written a couple of those articles myself, and now this book in which I hope to show you, my readers, why calling a professional is the right way to solve your decorating dilemmas and satisfy your dreams of living with beautiful colors, fabrics, window treatments, furnishings, lighting, and more.

The professionals I know best are my colleagues at Decorating Den—the brand name my husband Jim and I inherited when we bought into this franchise business idea in 1984. It seemed clear enough at the time, but the name came with its own baggage of misunderstandings. For some reason that we have yet to determine, it pleases our friends, no matter how many times we tell them otherwise, to call us DecoratORS Den. Even more disconcerting is the way many people assume all we decorate is dens. Adding "Interiors by" to the name is our latest attempt at clarifying the vast scope of our services.

In spite of the problematical pronunciation and misconception of Donayre, Bugg, and Interiors by Decorating Den, each of these associations has supplied the pizzazz to my decorating odyssey the way *passementrie* (ornamental trim) enriches ordinary draperies.

Discussing decorator Lauren Riddiough's (left) Dream Room entry with me and her mother Linda, who was one of my first franchise owners after joining Decorating Den twenty-four years ago.

Acknowledgments

*T*he purpose for writing this book was to enlighten the reader about what it is like to work with an interior decorator. My thanks to all of Decorating Den's talented decorators who provided the captivating Dream Room pictures and stories for this book. Equal appreciation goes to our smart clients who not only saw the value of using a professional to decorate their homes, but who also allowed us to photograph the results for all of the world to see.

I am indebted for the help of my colleagues at Decorating Den Corporate in rounding up photos and data, and in particular Melanie Jakab who advised me on certain pertinent content.

My thanks to my publisher Kathleen Hughes for seeing the value of producing a decorating book geared to the non do-it-yourselfer, and who so enthusiastically took on the project as editor, advisor, and staunch supporter. I am also pleased that Kathleen put me in touch with the vibrant book designer, Suzanne Stanton, who made my vision for "Decorating...*the professional touch*" even better than I anticipated.

*The view across the infilade
of rooms along the front of
my home.*

Introduction

What's A Decorator Got To Do With It?

A delightful fly fishing trip my husband and I once took on the river running through the majestic Cascade Mountain Loop in northeast Washington State reminds me about the value of seeking the help of a professional. Our lack of familiarity with these waters and a desire to make the most of our vacation prompted us to hire a fishing guide. Jim and I stopped at a local sporting goods store where we asked the owner for a recommendation, which led us to Chad. "If there are fish out there, he'll find them," the man praised his referral. The first catch of the day turned out to be Chad.

Our guide's immediate call to action was to learn something about us—our level of fly-fishing experience, and our expectations for the day ahead. Once he determined these, Chad collected the appropriate rods, reels, and bait, and the three of us set out in his boat.

I am always anxious when we go out with a new guide, wondering about his skill, or whether he will be one of those intimidating, know-it-alls. Some guides we have hired have been more interested in catching their own fish. But once I observed Chad's alert maneuvering down the shallow rapids, I felt confident his skill would keep us away from the dangerous rocks lurking ahead of us. I also sensed he was there to look out for our interests and see that we snagged trout.

After we had been out for a while luring only some small fish, Chad aimed his boat towards the riverbank. He was paddling along when suddenly I saw Jim's arm lurch back as his line took a hit. Before I knew it, Chad had jumped out of the boat shouting with glee, "You've hooked a steelhead!" Our delighted guide held the boat against the current, preventing it from going further downstream and getting the line tangled in the rocks. Chad was yelling words of encouragement to his client, making clear that this was going to be a team effort. The strenuous part of holding the boat would be left in Chad's capable hands. The joy of reeling in a prized steelhead salmon was up to my husband. Exhaustion turned to exhilaration for both men as Jim brought in their catch.

*The fishing guide's
expertise led Jim to catching a
prized steelhead salmon.*

THE LOUVRE

THE MUSÉE D'ORSAY

Like any successful collaboration, all parties involved in this expedition were elated with the outcome. Chad was ecstatic at having been able to provide us with a successful fishing trip, and Jim and I were thrilled to have had such an agreeable day, one that went even better than we had anticipated. The knowledge of the area and personal attention of our skilled guide increased the enjoyment and ease that had eluded us the times before when we had tried to go it alone.

How Decorating Your Home Can Be Like Our Fishing Success

Like our Cascade fishing trip, the process of decorating a home should be a pleasurable adventure– a little daring and a little different but one that ultimately results in expectations not simply being met, but surpassed. The difference between our fishing trip and furnishing a home is that in the end all we had left was a memory. But with decorating, the beautiful results are there to be enjoyed everyday.

An important consideration when seeking the help of an interior decorator is: Are you looking for an idea person, or a doer with ideas? When I was interviewing landscapers to do my front yard, I spoke to several individuals who charged hefty fees for doing the design, but let me know that they did not go beyond giving me a plan. In other words, getting the work done was up to me. Many interior decorators prefer to simply supply a design plan, but want nothing to do with the work of measuring, ordering, receiving, delivery, and installation. A good decorator—like those at Interiors by Decorating Den—takes pride in providing an all-encompassing design service, and our decorators receive great satisfaction in being the catalyst that brings your vision to life.

The client makeovers shown on the following pages originated as entries in IDD's annual Dream Rooms Contest. It is not important to point out the judges' choices because they are all winners with their clients. In fact, what separates Interiors by Decorating Den decorators from the others in their field is the relationship they enjoy with their clients. Frequently at our Dream Room awards ceremony, when the decorators come up on stage to talk about their projects, they add, "Oh, I can't wait to call my client and tell her that her room has won!"

Nothing is so fatiguing as the eternal
hanging on of an uncompleted task.
—William James

Until this book, I had forgotten all of the steps needed to update a room and prepare for a photo shoot. After my recent experiences in preparation for this book, I have a new admiration for what IDD decorators—and all good designers—do to beautify the lives of their clients and the extra effort they make in having their rooms professionally photographed.

The Decorator as a Facilitator

Considering the daunting prospect of decorating a home alone, of having to make all of the decisions regarding colors, fabrics, wallcoverings, window treatments, upholstered pieces, furniture, rugs, and lighting; then ordering, waiting for deliveries, and installation—is it any wonder that people delay decorating their homes?

Think of an interior decorator as your personal facilitator, with the ultimate mission to guide you to the most direct and pleasing conclusion. In the business world, a facilitator keeps everyone on track, guides random ideas, stimulates discussion, asks thought-provoking questions, and offers suggestions. I believe that

Photographer Gordon Beall
and me setting up for shooting
different views of my master
bedroom.

every homeowner––no matter how modest a residence or budget––deserves not only the services and sources of an interior decorator, but their advice and encouragement. Here is what you should expect from an interior decorator.

Preliminary . . . The Phone Call

During the initial phone conversation with the decorator she will introduce herself and ask you a few questions in preparation for the complimentary consultation in your home.

Please note: To simplify matters I will refer to the decorator as "she" because Interiors by Decorating Den is a 98 percent women dominated business.

Step One . . . The Appointment

The most convenient, time saving, and effective appointments take place in the client's home. Here you have the undistracted attention of the decorator, while she has the opportunity to observe you in your natural environment. It is discovery time for both parties. The decorator will show you her portfolio and explain how she works with clients. At the time of the first appointment you might be interested in making over one room, but giving the decorator a tour of your home will provide her with a better understanding of how you use your entire house.

The decorator will want to know your everyday habits, such as:

- Where you prefer to eat your meals; breakfast in bed, dinner in front of the flat screened TV in the great room?

- How you like to entertain: formal dinner parties, casual family gatherings, or a bit of both?

- Are there certain furnishings that you cannot part with: your piano, desk, or favorite chair?

- What items are you willing to let go, hand down to the children, donate to charity, or discard because they are beyond repair? And so on.

The decorator's intention is to get to know you, so that she can create a home that reflects the colors, style, and mood that appeals to you and your family.

Depending on the scope of the job, an initial appointment can last from a couple hours to many. This gives the decorator sufficient time to collect all the necessary information, take some measurements, study window exposures, make notations on the items she needs to work around, and take pictures to use as a reference when she is back in her studio designing your project.

At the end of the first meeting, the decorator will clarify what you have discussed so far, and ask for a budget range that you feel comfortable with. She will set a date for the next appointment. Everyone involved in the decision making process should plan to be included when the decorator returns to present her ideas.

Step Two . . . The Return of the Decorator

Between steps one and two, the decorator devises a plan and researches products that reflect your individual taste. When she returns to your home for the much-anticipated second appointment, the decorator will be fortified with swatches, samples, and color schemes, explaining the reasons and thought process behind her comprehensive design plan. She will listen to your concerns, and make adjustments where needed. Once you and the decorator are in agreement, she will provide you with a contract detailing the items to be ordered, offer payment options, and give you approximate delivery dates. The ordering process is then set in motion.

Step Three . . . Custom Orders

I tend to boast that all of the rooms in this book are sensations . . . just not "overnight" sensations! There is no getting around the fact that custom, made-to-order furnishings take longer to produce than something bought "as is" off the floor. Each sofa and loveseat you order is upholstered in your personal choice of fabric, the finish of every table and chair has been specified by you, and your draperies are designed to coordinate with the style and colors of the room and custom fabricated to fit the size of the windows.

All of this takes time, and depending on the variables, somewhere between four weeks to four months, but most often somewhere in between. In the interim, walls can be painted or papered, carpet can be removed, and floors can be refinished. During this time, your decorator will keep you apprised of the progress of furniture being received at her warehouse, and notify you of any unexpected delays.

Step Four . . . The Grand Finale

When the day finally arrives, I advise a client to leave her house and allow the decorator to go to work delivering and arranging the new furniture, placing the accessories, and installing the window treatments. You will have one of the most thrilling experiences of your lifetime when you return home and see your new window treatment or revitalized room, for the very first time.

Why seek an interior decorator?
Because a decorator accepts
responsibility for your project
from concept to completion as
Sally Giar did for the Corbett's
family room shown in this
storyboard.

12 Incentives for Seeking the Help of an Interior Decorator

1. Because a decorator brings expertise to the overwhelming prospect of you trying to do it by yourself.

2. Because a decorator will save you the time and hassle of going from store to store, and will come to your home and work around your furnishings and in your lighting.

3. Because a decorator has unlimited access to "to-the-trade" resources that will satisfy all of your home furnishing needs.

4. Because a decorator narrows down the abundance of selections in each product category to the ones that best fit your situation.

5. Because a decorator can spare you from making costly mistakes.

6. Because a decorator attends to all of the details required when placing orders that consumers are not even aware of.

7. Because a decorator knows how to design, measure, and order each category of home furnishings, as well as organize all deliveries and installations.

8. Because a decorator can easily determine what products will best integrate with the furnishings you already have.

9. Because a decorator has the ability to mesh the individual tastes of husbands and wives and come up with a beautiful compromise that pleases both parties.

10. Because a decorator can custom design a window treatment, a room, or your entire home and you will only be charged for the products you decide to buy.

11. Because a decorator accepts responsibility for your project from concept to completion.

12. Because a decorator can take your ideas and make them even better.

There is no better way to explain the process of working with an interior decorator than to show you. Beginning with the unique story in chapter three, *DECORATING . . . the professional touch* is full of real life examples of what a decorator can do for you.

So relax, and use this book to get ideas for what you want in your home, and then pick up the phone and call a decorator to get "the professional touch" they can bring to your home decorating dreams.

One Decorator's Path to a Lifelong Career

I begin this book with my own journey in the world of interior design. It is my hope that the story of my continuing career path will be an inspiration to those readers who have a similar passion and will motivate them to follow their dream of being an interior decorator.

I never tired of seeing this view as we approached Manhattan from the Queensboro Bridge.

Some mothers home school their kids. Mine deferred reading, writing, and arithmetic to the nuns; but as early as I can remember, she was schooling my sister Jeanne and me in the nuances of interior decorating. My true inheritance is being able to claim that mecca of creative energy, Manhattan, as my earliest training ground, and Mother as my first design teacher.

A main step for achieving enlightenment is to discover your right livelihood. —Budda

Chapter 1

My Interior Decorating Odyssey

She would never have been so presumptuous as to compare herself to another Brooklyn born, self-taught woman named Elsie de Wolfe, who during the same era was elevating the decoration of houses into a profession, defining good design as "suitability, suitability, suitability." But the truth is, I learned more about interior decorating from my mother than from any of my later teachers.

Three months after I was born in Brooklyn, Mother got her wish and we moved to the "urban suburbia" of Jackson Heights in Queens. It was one of the first American neighborhoods specifically created as a garden apartment community. Of more relevance to Mother than the bucolic setting was in knowing she could be over the Queensboro Bridge and in her beloved Manhattan in less than an hour. In *The Great Gatsby*, F. Scott Fitzgerald described how I felt each time we approached Manhattan, "The city seen from the Queensboro Bridge is always the city seen for the first time, in its first wild promise of all the mystery and beauty in the world."

Our promenades down Fifth Avenue began at 57th Street, one of the world's prime intersections long before Donald Trump built his tower over that corner. Window-shopping with Mother was a series of impromptu lessons on the elements of design. Her tutorials alerted me to the way line, form, scale, color, and texture play a part in creating pleasing environments.

I have a vivid recollection of one window in particular, where without the help of mannequins the stylist had managed to flesh out an enviable homey setting. He had made it possible for onlookers to imagine a couple enjoying a leisurely Sunday morning reading the newspaper. Discarded sections of the *New York Times* were scattered about on an Oriental rug. There were crushed cigarettes in ashtrays, two half-filled cups of coffee, the remains of partially eaten sweet rolls, and a barely filled-in crossword puzzle, all randomly placed across an eclectic mix of tables.

The sofa and chair pillows remained indented as if the occupants had recently left the room. The telephone receiver was off the hook, a hint at what the couple might be up to, but a detail Mother failed to point out. I was just beginning to notice things like that, but was still too young to appreciate the full extent of how the stylist's alluring *mise en scene* was designed to entice window voyeurs into the store so they could replicate this charmed lifestyle in their own homes.

My grandson Brady mesmerized as I, in the style of my mother, explain the exquisite details of a Christmas window designed by Linda Fargo for Bergdorf Goodman.

Cruising the furniture floors of department stores like Lord & Taylor, John Wanamakers, and B. Altman & Company further cultivated my curiosity for interior decorating. Each season Lord & Taylor's legendary decorator, William Pahlmann, came up with a set of stunning new model rooms. What made Pahlmann's decorating so appealing was his belief that, "Good decoration is a design for the living, not for looking. It is the service of human needs." When Pahlman introduced Swedish-modern furniture to the American public, Mother fell in love with the sleek, blond-wood look. She was determined to find a way to weave light contemporary furnishings in with the dark, traditional pieces she and my father had settled on when they were first married.

The most comprehensive exhibition of interior decorating was to be found in the two-story show house constructed inside W. & J. Sloane's flagship furniture store on Fifth Avenue. One day we watched as an interior decorator put the finishing touches on the living room. I stood in awe as she arranged a group of accessories on a table, moving each item multiple times until the composition suited her vision.

On another occasion Mother asked about a piece of furniture she had seen on display, and the smartly dressed young woman asked us to follow her back to her design studio. Her office was divinely cluttered. There were bolts of gorgeous fabrics stacked upright in the corners of the room, and sets of blueprints stashed in a tall metal umbrella stand. An inspiration bulletin board pinned with fascinating pictures and clips of samples covered most of one wall. Spread out across her desk were fans of paint chips, fabric swatches, and opened wallpaper books. The young woman apologized to Mother for the mess, explaining that she was in the process of making selections for a client's home. To my young eyes the decorator's disorderly space was much more appealing than the pristine organization of my father's office.

When we were not gawking at model rooms and design studios, we were studying the set decorations at the movies. In hushed tones Mother would draw our attention to some tempting detail that caught her sharp eyes. She was particularly taken with the urbane surroundings created by MGM's art director, Cedric Gibbons, a name that became as familiar to me as any movie star of the day. On the bus ride back to Jackson Heights Mother relived each scene, exclaiming over an elegant drapery treatment, or the shape of a sofa arm, in the same way my husband after each golf game replays his birdie putts, or the length of a great drive.

I remember how my mother took the mundane rooms of our apartment and turned them into places of quiet beauty. She had a knack for combining a few good things with some inexpensive finds. Mother was always after a "look" and adroit enough to figure out how to achieve it without having things costing, as she would say, "an arm and a leg."

There was an incident when Mother found a way around Daddy's reluctance to buy a new sofa and chair because he felt what we owned was in perfectly good condition. That was not going to stop the "work-around" queen of Queens from updating our living room with the more subdued tones being promoted on the sets of chic Hollywood films, and in the trendy model rooms of New York's finest stores.

My handsome father and lovely mother captured with my Kodak Brownie camera the day I graduated from grammar school.

My father, who had been appointed Minister Commercial Counselor for the Peruvian Embassy, was now living in Washington D.C. during the week. Waiting until Daddy was out of town, Mother arranged to have our Louis XV style sofa and chairs stripped, stained, and reupholstered. In her decision to exchange the sedate ruby velvet for a smart sage texture, and lightening the dark mahogany frame to a more fashionable blond stain, my mother was either extremely confident, or very daring, or both.

Edward Durell Stone covered his New York City brownstone with his signature grille design.

Along with my burgeoning fascination for furniture and fashion, I was attracted to architecture. One could not spend time in New York City and be indifferent towards its astonishing skyscrapers, grand hotels, and the majestic Rockefeller Center. My father promoted this interest when he introduced us to architect Edward Durell Stone. Stone, considered a foremost interpreter of the International Style initiated by Germany's Bauhaus School, was Daddy's choice to design and build one of the largest hospitals in the world in Lima, Peru.

I must admit at the time I was more impressed with Mr. Stone's car and his girlfriend than I was with his esteemed reputation. Indelible in my memory are two occasions: the Saturday Mr. Stone, and his friend Gwen Lux, picked us up in his sporty convertible to take us to Jones Beach, and the evening we visited Ms. Lux, a sculptor of renown, in her brilliant sky-lit studio in the West 40s. Both times I thought I had died and gone to Hollywood heaven.

Edward Durell Stone's renown escalated after he was commissioned to design the Kennedy Center in Washington D.C. But, in architectural circles he is recognized for his signature Arabesque grille, first used on the façade of the U.S. Pavillion at

the 1958 Brussels World's Fair and then at the U.S. Chancellery in New Delhi.

In a *Time Magazine* interview, Stone described the dual purpose of the grille as, "Not only satisfying a wistful yearning on the part of everyone for pattern, warmth and interest, but it also serves the desperately utilitarian purpose of keeping the sun off glass and giving privacy." Later I came to appreciate how every architect and designer of worth employs the concept of form and function in their work. After Stone sheathed the façade of his Upper East Side brownstone residence with the grille design, neighbors strongly objected, but today the building is designated a New York City Landmark.

My mother's memory of Ed Stone would more likely have revolved around his having a hand in decorating our apartment. Getting his seal of approval made it easier for Mother to convince my father that incorporating modern blond furniture in with our existing traditional furnishing was acceptable. Stone's introduction to the timeless designs of T. H. Robsjohn-Gibbings for John Widdicomb provided us with the dining room furniture that my sister Jeanne continues to use and enjoy to this day.

Once we joined my father in Washington, D.C., Mother and her conglomeration of furnishings did quite well transitioning from a city apartment to our suburban home. It was during these teenage years, in our new environs, that I expanded my design and architecture vocabulary to include the likes of Mt. Vernon, the White House, and Georgetown's Federal town homes. And with my own money saved from a summer job, plus a little help from my father's wallet, I also experienced making a furniture purchase for myself.

A timeless piece of furniture that had a place in my teenage bedroom, my apartment dining room, and endures in its current place at our lodge in the country.

At first winding my way by myself through the aisles of the bedroom section of a furniture store, I was disappointed not to find the piece I had in mind. I detoured into the area allocated to dining room case goods, and it was there I spotted a modestly scaled, transitionally styled fruitwood buffet/credenza with the exact dimensions allowed for my small bedroom, and with enough space for storing clothing and housing my collection of LP records.

My premiere venture into buying furniture taught me to ignore room labels, and educated me to the fact that in the long run it pays to invest in quality pieces. This buffet/credenza was of no particular period and therefore fit in with other styles without going out of style itself. When I moved into my first apartment, the buffet went with me, finding its proper place in my dining room amid my switch to more contemporary furnishings. The reason I recall this early purchase so well is because I see it every time we visit our house in the country.

Finding my true profession took a circuitous route after I decided not to conform to the marrying path of my classmates graduating from Georgetown Visitation Junior College. Instead I was subjected to a variety of beige-collar jobs. The day came when my constant bitching about the boring work as a receptionist in a law firm drove one exasperated secretary to yell in my face, "Why don't you shut up and do something about it!"

I don't know whether it was the result of her prayers or simply my predestination, but shortly after this encounter the *Washington Star* newspaper carried a full-page article about the International Institute of Interior Design (IIID). Until reading the story, I was unaware that such a professional school existed locally. One look at the curriculum and I knew I had found relief for my receptionist blues.

The Newspaper Article that Influenced My Decision to Attend Design School

After I traded my receptionist desk for a drafting table at IIID, I approached each class and assignment with uncustomary fervor. I did not recall ever taking such immense pleasure in reading textbooks. I discovered I could become a student of history if it related to architecture and the decorative arts. In the past I faulted myself for not having a good memory; but when it came to design, I retained even the smallest of details. I was delighted to learn the principles behind my view-it-by-eye sense of scale, balance, and line. I relished

The Washington Star *article that sent me off to design school.*

gaining insight into the fundamentals of textile weaving and wallpaper printing. I was fascinated by the psychology and theory of color. I also found I had a talent for furniture arranging, drafting floor plans, and rendering perspectives. And whatever profession one chooses, it is a must to relate to the tools of one's trade. I was enamored with my T-squares, triangles, and templates.

For three years at the International Institute of Interior Design I immersed myself in color charts, floor plans, art history, textiles, and furniture. I learned to be draftsman, designer, and estimator; but the day came when I had to step out of the classroom comfort zone and get some hands-on experience. Part of my decision to leave IIID before I completed the program was due to losing my mentor, my beloved mother. Unlike my father who had passed away before I started design school, she at least was able to share those happy days with me. What would have truly pleased her was where I landed my first interior design job.

I was hired as a draftsman at W. & J. Sloane, not in the Fifth Avenue store where my interest in interior decorating had been primed by my mother, but at their branch in Washington, D.C. The salary was less than I had been making as a receptionist at the law firm, but the name W. & J. Sloane on my design resume would be a valuable credential. What I learned at IIID was nothing compared with the design education I was about to receive on the job.

Dressed in my best black suit, I went to Sloane's that first day feeling every bit the interior decorator, but like the bible prediction about pride, the hubris was knocked out of me when I was directed to punch a time clock. I was appalled. Don't blue-collar workers punch time clocks?! In spite of the humbling start and end of each day, I plunged enthusiastically into my work. I delighted in the interaction with my more experienced co-workers, who were most generous in sharing their knowledge with the new kid at the drafting table. The advantage of starting out at Sloane's was I had no place to go but up. A year later that chance opened up.

I heard through my peer grapevine that the respected Baltimore design firm, The H. Chambers Company, was opening up a satellite office in Washington, D.C. I called and obtained an interview with Lee Chambers' wife, Kit. My design school education and work experience seemed to satisfy the requirements for whatever position Mrs. Chambers had in mind for me, but she wanted to know more. Those were the days when inquiries into the personal life of a potential employee were acceptable.

Not trusting my bare ring finger Kit Chambers asked, "Are you engaged?" "No," I replied. She probed further, "Are you dating anyone?" "No," I sadly, but honestly admitted.

I understood the concern of the boss's wife about turnover, and was pleased that my responses provided her with the assurance that I would be a steady employee. When Mrs. Chambers offered me the chance to be part of the D. C. team, I was elated, but only momentarily. She then proceeded to inform me that the only position not yet filled was the receptionist job. I was beyond disappointment at having to take two steps backwards, but the choice was mine. I decided to view it as career advancement. The offer of double my Sloane's salary, and no longer having to punch a time clock would offset the lesser job title.

Besides it was a privilege to be associated with this well respected design firm, and to learn my trade firsthand from Lee Chambers and the other top designers his company attracted. Even though The H. Chambers Company drew a high-end clientele, Lee always stressed that no matter the budget of the account, it was the designer's "professional obligation to steer clients away from pitfalls and lead them to an overall design which will both work for them and please them."

Along with the artistic facet of interior decorating, I was equally attracted to the business side of design. It is one thing to be an interior decorator, quite another to run a design business. Chamber's office staff was small enough for me to be involved in all aspects of opening up a design studio and showroom. I assisted the manager, was a girl Friday to the senior decorators, and helped the design assistant with cross referencing catalogs and establishing a fabric library. Along with all my former work experiences, I filed these skills away for future reference.

In a matter of months The H. Chambers Company's D.C. business was booming, and I was out of a receptionist job. I had advanced to assistant decorator. Luck was in my favor when I went to work at Chambers, not simply on the career side, but in the short time the staff was together we had become one small happy office family. Nevertheless, I yearned to be as fortunate in the personal side of my life.

My wish was to come true, and the long-term relationship Kit Chambers had counted on turned out to be as fleeting as a one-season fad. I met and three months later married Jim Bugg, the man who added that touch of whimsy to my name, not to mention my life.

Jim became my new boss as I took on the responsibilities of designing boutiques for his Jacques Renee franchise company. When he sold the company and we moved to St. Louis, I worked as an interior decorator for Stix, Baer & Fuller, a fine family owned department store. It was here that I enjoyed the satisfaction decorators feel when they help create a dream home for an appreciative client. I also was given the chance to work on several commercial projects. Stix had an impressive training program where all employees were indoctrinated into the founders' service-oriented philosophy. Like many stores of that ilk and time that catered to their clients, Stix, Baer & Fuller is out of business. I regret that today's discount obsessed consumers rarely encounter the kind of service, courtesy, and pampering offered by the great department stores of old.

Ultimately, we moved back to the Washington, D.C. area where Jim got involved with Century 21 and real estate franchising, and I ventured into model home decorating.

I learned right away that this type of decorating was fast paced, riddled with unpredictable situations, and unrealistic deadlines rarely met by developers. Schedules were subject to erratic weather conditions, no-show subcontractors (especially during deer season), and a general pile-up of workers in each other's way that last week before the builder's grand opening. But, with all of the headaches associated with model home decorating—deadlines, delays, and deer—I determined that I really loved doing models and the sense of accomplishment that comes from wrapping up a project. In time I opened up my own business. Louis Pasteur said, "Chance favors the prepared mind," and that was the case of how I acquired my richest model home job project.

Jim and I have this thing about missing each other at airports, so in general we find it more expedient to cab it home. But one summer night I put the top down on my convertible and drove out to Dulles Airport on the chance that we would find each other. I always take immense pleasure in approaching Dulles and seeing Eero Saarinen's stunning structure, one of the few modern architectural masterpieces in the metro Washington D.C. area.

After an apprehensive fifteen minutes of intense looking, I finally spotted Jim coming in my direction, but he was not alone. He introduced me to Michael Gulino, his seat companion on the plane whom he had offered to give a ride home. Jim explained that Mr. Gulino was in charge of Hillandale, a new townhouse project in Georgetown, adding with a big grin, "Michael would like to talk to you about decorating his model home."

I was familiar with the magnificent Mediterranean style Archibold Estate that was the site for Hillandale. The main residence sat high on a knoll surrounded by 42 acres of rolling hills with grazing sheep that had been visible from our hockey field during my days at Georgetown Visitation. Clint Murchison, owner of the Dallas Cowboys, had bought the land and put Michael Gulino in charge of developing the property into townhouses for Hillandale at Georgetown.

By the time my husband introduced me to Gulino, ground had been broken, the foundations for the first section were in, and all of the major players had been cast except for the interior decorator. An introduction like the one Jim had given me was good for one audition. When I had my chance, I gave the presentation performance of my life and got the part of decorating the model at Hillandale.

The downside of the contract was that Gulino had chosen to decorate the hardest-to-sell floor plan, albeit a smart decision on his part when there is only one model designated to be furnished. My job was to come up with a design scheme that would make the sole model appealing to the affluent, sophisticated, and well-traveled prospective buyer profile. To reach this market required using the finest fabrics, wallcoverings, furniture, and accessories, which called for a buying trip to New York, not that I needed an excuse to return to Manhattan. I was on the hunt not only for product, but for inspiration.

My greatest challenge was showing prospects how they could adjust to downsizing from a large home to a townhouse. My plan was to visually maximize the use of the limited floor space, and make them feel comfortable in smaller spaces, such as the living room which was barely 12 feet wide. Also of concern in the living room was the huge window that ran the full height and almost the entire length of the two-story wall. The choice of fabric was crucial. It needed to soften and enhance without overpowering the window, or distracting from the lovely wooded view outside.

I selected an exquisite Jack Lenor Larsen textured sheer with a horizontal burnout chevron pattern to downplay the strong vertical lines and overwhelming dimensions of the window. The main feature of my window design was a deep eyebrow arched cornice hung over traversing drapery panels. If ever a window treatment called for George Evans, my expert window installer, it was this one.

When we were still a couple of weeks away from the "Grand Opening," Michael received a call from *The Washington Dossier*, a local society magazine. The editor wanted to include a picture of the Hillandale model in an upcoming issue, but the deadline was NOW! If the model had not been so near completion, we would have missed this perfect public relations opportunity.

Publicity from the Hillandale project led to more model home jobs, and a commission from the Singapore Embassy to furnish homes intended for their diplomatic staff. My business was thriving, but Jim had retired and was spending much of his time at Poverty Point, our country place on the Eastern Shore of Maryland.

The issue of Woman's Day that launched Jim and me into Decorating Den.

When the time is right, we can count on luck, fortune, chance, destiny, whatever one chooses to call it, to make an appearance. On a balmy day in early April 1984 my husband responded to a "Walk-ins Welcome" sign in the window of a unisex hair salon. Upon welcoming Jim home I pretended not to notice his spring sheering, but it was harder to overlook his bursting excitement to share his latest discovery. He related how the only magazine left for him to read while he waited for a stylist was *Woman's Day*. The probability of my husband discovering something he could relate to in the pages of *Woman's Day* was about as remote as my identifying with the swimsuit issue of *Sports Illustrated*.

Jim shoved the magazine into my hands and waited impatiently as I read an article about the franchise company, Decorating Den. When I accused Jim of stealing the salon's magazine, he assured me he had purchased his own copy at the drugstore. To him the fact that the issue was current was an additional sign of fate. It was evident that Jim's rapture over the article came from viewing the concept of running an interior decorating business out of a van as the missing link to a notion we had been kicking about for years. Combining Jim's franchise expertise with my design experience, and starting an interior decorating franchise had always seemed an appropriate venture for us; but we had failed to come up with an original way of promoting it. Jim was taken with Decorating Den's premise of a franchise not tied to a storefront and with the vision of decorators going directly to customer's homes.

I became a fan of Decorating Den when I recognized we shared the same opinion about interior decorating–that it is a service and should be accessible and affordable for everyone to enjoy. Five years prior, in response to articles in the trade publication *Designer Magazine*, I wrote a letter to the editor.

As a model home interior decorator, and a professional making a living, I was gratified to read your editorial four/79, along with articles, "The Designer As Merchandiser" and "Not Every Client Is A Millionaire." So many of my colleagues assume the attitude that a professional designer works only with the affluent client. These designers' budgets for doing a job overwhelm the vast market of middle-income people. You are right when you say that interior design is a service. A person should be able to hire a decorator who, for a realistic budget, is able to provide the client with

beauty, comfort, and good design. The best definition of a designer that I have heard is, "One who creates beauty." No more should working with a designer to "create beauty" be the domain of the rich alone.

Every so often a person, a team, or a company comes along and proves that no matter what the trade–decorating, fashion, architecture, movies, etc–it is possible to produce something beautiful and worthwhile for a reasonable amount of money.

A perfect example in the field of films is the legendary movie producing team of Merchant/Ivory. Frugality did not prevent them from turning out the most exquisite, universally appealing, and award-winning moving pictures of the last century (*Remains of the Day*, *Howard's End*). In an industry known for overblown egos and ridiculous cost overruns, they set the example for keeping costs in line, knowing where to cut back, and coming up with ways to exploit existing scenery and properties, rather than developing everything from the ground up.

In the arena of interior decorating where outlandish estimates, starting from scratch, and decorator dictators are often the norm, promoting the attitude of working around people's furnishings, supplying them with what they want, and keeping within a realistic budget made Decorating Den the exception. There was no doubt that this was a business that suited Jim's and my views and experience. I was thrilled that my husband was looking into a business that might possibly exit him out of his premature retirement. Personally, I was caught up in my own plans.

As a student in Paris, sitting at my desk in my tres, tres, petite single room.

Each spring I received a brochure announcing the Parsons School of Design's summer program in Paris. In the past I relied on the usual bag of excuses for not going. I don't have the time. I don't have the money. I don't want to be separated from the man in my life. This was the year I made up my mind to make the time, find the money, and grab the chance to be on my own. The Parsons program would not only get me back to Paris, but allow me to experience my fantasy of living there as a student, albeit a senior one.

Familiarity with the layout of Paris, a Metro pass, and my garret-sized room on the Left Bank eased me into the Parisian lifestyle. Each morning fortified with coffee and croissant, we toured the city listening to our engaging professor bring alive the structures and former inhabitants of centuries old edifices, churches, and neighborhoods. In the afternoon, following a leisurely two-hour break for lunch, the group reassembled at the Louvre's Musee des Art Decoratifs, where another distinguished professor lectured us on French interiors, furnishings, and the decorative arts.

My darling husband called me daily, sometimes in the middle of the night when he forgot the time difference, or when he could not wait until morning to reveal his enthusiasm for the latest bit of positive information that he had uncovered about Decorating Den.

We were both having the time of our lives, but on two different continents.

When my Parsons school days were coming to an end, I feared post-Paris depression, but Jim was already making plans so I would not have a free moment to feel blue. By the time I returned home, our getting involved with Decorating Den was a fait accompli.

*P*res and après Decorating Den is the way I define my continuing interior decorating odyssey. It was as if all those prior years were preparation for the day I became Director of Design for Decorating Den. I finally had an outlet for relaying my accumulated knowledge and experience, and sharing my passion for interior decorating with kindred spirits.

From right to left, Carol,
Linda Riddiough, Dana Hayman,
Patti Coons performing during talent
night at Dec Den's convention at the
Opryland Hotel.

The Decorators Who Come to Your Home and Listen to Your Ideas

There have been a few important changes since Jim and I bought into the Decorating Den concept. At different points along the way, we became the owners of the company; three of our children, Jimmy, Darlene and Whitney, joined us in the business; then to better clarify the scope of services the name was changed to Interiors by Decorating Den (IDD); and several years ago we moved our headquarters and training center to Easton, Maryland.

With those facts out of the way, I can proceed with the saga.

It is a well-known fact that the majority of people would rather face a tax audit than an audience. I was not an exception. I thought the best thing about graduating from fourteen years of Catholic school was that I was finished with nuns forcing me to get up and speak in front of large groups of people. What I never imagined was that there would come a time when I'd step out of my comfort zone and stand at podiums and in front of television cameras sounding off about some facet of interior decorating.

My first television appearance was filmed at the High Point Furniture Market, from a perched position inside our rainbow trademarked white van, explaining our service to Nancy Foreman on NBC's *Today Show*. She began the segment pointing out the most noteworthy trends shown at the market, and ended with, "After fifty-five acres of home furnishings you might wonder how to put it all together. Well, help is on the way. Decorating Den is equipped for any interior design challenge." That interview set in motion a variety of appearances on other network and cable shows. Broadcast media is endlessly fascinated by the Dec Den story, both as a franchise

opportunity and as the pleasant alternative for busy women who do not have the time, nor the desire, to do-it-themselves.

Throughout the years, my responsibilities have been vast and varied, but one of the most satisfying is my involvement with Decorating Den's Dream Room Contest. The competition was an in-house event before Patti Coons came on board as our director of communications. She had the good sense to upgrade the event to New York City and invite the editors of the major shelter, women's, and trade publications to be the judges. The contest became an unprecedented opportunity for Dec Den interior decorators to have their work brought to the attention of the media.

A story worth repeating is about the year we moved the Dream Room Contest to New York City's Plaza Hotel. By then I had overcome my fear of speaking in public, especially when addressing our franchise owners, or making a presentation to an audience at a decorating workshop. But that cold spring morning I was intimidated looking out at the crème de la crème from the home fashion media: Lou Gropp, *House Beautiful*; Charles Gandee, *House & Garden*; Joe Ruggierio, *Home Magazine*; and Kitty Bartholomew, *The ABC Home Show*.

I stood before them on a raised platform, clutching the podium, making every effort to appear relaxed and confident. It was unlike me not to have a speech prepared weeks in advance, but shortly before I faced this elite group the message I wanted to convey suddenly became clear.

Good morning, and thank you for joining us to judge Decorating Den's Dream Room Contest. I did not always think of Decorating Den as a trendsetting company, but as I was preparing my talk to you today I realized we are on the cutting edge of many trends.

When it comes to residential design, the perception of the bored housewife client is out, and the busy career woman is in. Many interior designers disdain working with the residential client. They explain how they cannot tolerate the indecisive, time-on-her-hands lady of the house.

My friends, that scenario is out-of-date. What these designers have failed to recognize is that today's busy career woman does not want to waste her time any more than they do. In addition, she earns her own money, and no longer needs her husband's approval to spend it.

Decorating Den enjoys doing business with this neglected niche market. We love dealing with the new savvy female consumer, and they in turn love our approachable, convenient, and affordable decorating service. We thank the snobby interior designers for leaving "those people," as one of my colleagues referred to Decorating Den's clientele, to us.

After you study the Dream Room Contest boards, tell me if you think what these decorators have done has not been important to improving the lives of ordinary people, and are not "these people" deserving of our decorating services?

As a result of the Dream Room Contest, Decorating Den was featured in a Charles Gandee column in House & Garden magazine.

Donald Trump, after hiring Decorating Den to update his Plaza Hotel's Presidential Suite, with (from left to right) Judith Slaughter, Carol, Patti Coons (standing), Jill Locke, and Carol's daughter Darlene.

Decorating Den is at the forefront of another hot trend, women are going into business for themselves at two and one-half times the rate of men. Decorating Den is a 98 percent woman-dominated business. For twenty years we have been training and providing support for women who not only want to be decorators, but who also want to own their own business.

God knows, Jim and I never imagined working so closely together in the same business, but husbands and wives actually wanting to work together are very much in vogue. Most of Decorating Den's regions are managed by couples. Many female franchisees start the business on their own, and then their husbands join them as partners.

So in the end, Decorating Den is very much on the cutting edge of some of this decade's hottest trends.

By noon the editors had chosen the winners and it was time for us to reward them for their efforts with lunch in the newly redecorated Edwardian Room of the Plaza. Our current Decorator of The Year also joined us. At the time Donald Trump owned the Plaza Hotel, and on that particular day he was entertaining several businessmen at "his" corner table, an opportunity not to be missed by our PR maven Patti.

When he finished his lunch, the affable Donald came by our table and gallantly posed for pictures with everyone. Even after the camera flashes stopped, he continued to chat with his captive audience. Trump was about to make his exit, when he turned to our Decorator of The Year and said, "A movie has just been shot in the Presidential Suite, and it has been totally trashed. I need someone to pull it back together in thirty days. Do you think you could do the job?"

My sister Jeanne and me posing in one of the newly redecorated bedrooms in the Presidential Suite of the Plaza Hotel.

Decorating Den was "hired" by The Donald to update his 12,000 square foot suite that we were told rented in 1992 for $15,000 a day. We were asked to work around the existing antiques, wallpaper, and the $300 per yard red damask that covered the living room walls. The size of the project and the contract might have been more substantial than Decorating Den's typical client, but the criteria of creating a beautiful environment, working around existing furnishings, and keeping within a budget remained the

IDD hosted a special wine tasting party at Mount Vernon.

Photos above, left to right: workshop, working the market, studying the Dream Room boards, on stage with Jim Bugg, Sr. and Jim Bugg, Jr; Awards Gala in Hyatt Ballroom; one of the groups of franchise owners who were recognized at the Awards Gala for their outstanding business achievements, conference attendees being entertained at the opening night party by Andy Childs.

same. Decorating the Presidential Suite at the Plaza Hotel was a tremendous coup, and resulted for many years in our returning to the Plaza where the Decorating Den staff and the latest Decorators of The Year stayed, and where we held the contest judging.

I cried the day I passed the Plaza Hotel in 2005 and saw it closed down and boarded up. The grand dame of hotels was in the process of being converted into a condominium/retail complex. The glory days of us staying in the Presidential Suite are over, but Decorating Den has moved the Decorator of The Year celebration to two other New York City landmarks, the Waldorf-Astoria Hotel and the Four Seasons Restaurant in the Seagram Building.

Both of these venues offer lessons in design—the Waldorf –Astoria with its turn-of-the-century elegance and the Four Seasons with its breathtaking interiors and furnishings by the architectural giant Ludwig Mies Van der Rohe. After a half a century his "less is more" philosophy, and his Barcelona and Brno chairs remain stunning examples of enduring icons. I dined there for the first time during my design school days. I was impressed then, but now on my return visits I have the added pleasure of sharing the cachet of the Four Seasons with my appreciative Decorating Den colleagues. And always on hand to lend bonhomie to the evening affair is our friend,

the charming and witty interior decorator, Mario Buatta. Mario has also graced us with his presence at three of our conferences.

My husband says it's okay to brag if it is true. Interiors by Decorating Den produces the grandest conventions. When they are over, we always wonder, "How are we going to top that next year?" Somehow we always seem to do so. Our conferences run the gamut of exciting cities and fabulous hotels: the Princess in Acapulco, Opryland in Nashville, the Riviera in Palm Springs, the Fontainebleau in Miami, the Dolphin in Orlando, and the Biltmore in Los Angeles, to name a few. But the real reason for the success of IDD conferences is our staff's reliable recipe of mixing equal parts of work and play.

Our decorators like to party and love doing so in the company of their old friends, but they also have an insatiable appetite for learning. They gravitate to our extensive supplier market to review the latest products, and are dedicated to continuing their education at pre-conference classes and workshops. They are interested in learning from the testimonies of their success panel peers, and they take pride in being recognized for their design and business achievements.

In addition to Mario Buatta, IDD has had its share of well-known speakers over the years at our conventions: author Dr. Joyce Brothers; and TV hosts Chris Madden and Kitty Bartholomew; *House Beautiful's* editor-in-chief Lou Gropp; Waverly Fabrics president Meri Stevens: cookie queen Mrs. Fields; *Passages* author Gail Sheehy, who during her talk continued to refer to us as DecoratORS Den; beautiful supermodel turned home furnishings product designer Kathy Ireland; and Bob Mackie (read his story in chapter fourteen).

Luisa Maringola (r.) and Marisa Lupo, longtime franchise partners from Canada, being entertained at the Four Seasons Restaurant by the delightful Mario Buatta and his trademark bug.

A request from the Congressional Club in Washington D.C. to select an appropriate fabric for their annual First Lady's Luncheon led to my collaborating with Meri Stevens, president of Waverly Fabrics, on an exclusive design for this event. The membership of the club is comprised of a bi-partisan group of women politically associated by marriage—the wives of congressmen, senators, members of the cabinet and the Supreme Court. The club's most important annual event is this luncheon, and a significant element of its success is the fabric chosen to cover the dais and 150 tables.

My all-American fabric design enhanced with pearls in honor of First Lady Barbara Bush.

Rather than pick an existing fabric, I offered to create an exclusive fabric for First Lady Barbara Bush. From the beginning I had a design in mind, but I was hesitant to go with my first idea before researching other options. In the end I returned to the original vision, which was a toile because traditionally the scenes depicted in its print commemorate particular people and events.

Thus evolved a romantic patriotic print comprised of flowering urns entwined in graceful scrolls, dotted with pearls, enhanced with eagles carrying the Stars and Stripes. The color scheme was All-American, but softened to a rosy red, bluebonnet blue, and pearly white with contrasting accents of green and gold. We named it "First lady Tribute," and Meri Stevens built an entire Waverly collection around the centerpiece fabric.

The premiere of this exclusive design was well received by the attendees at the Congressional Club's 1990 luncheon. *The Washington Post* covered the story with the headline in their Home Section, "First Lady Fabric a Bipartisan Hit:"

The ropes of pearls that have become First Lady Barbara Bush's signature are making the rounds of living and dining rooms of congress. The pearls are the focal point of a floral chintz that bedecks the homes of about two dozen congressional families on sofas, table skirts and window treatments.

At the begining of our beautiful friendship, Mario Buatta giving me a tour of one his Kips Bay Show House rooms.

Esther Coopersmith, a well-known Democratic fundraiser, fell in love with the "First Lady Tribute" and arranged to have it cover the tables of a gala fundraising dinner party in New York at Sothby's. Jim and I were introduced to many interesting people at this elegant affair, and that was the night that we established our long-lasting friendship with Mario Buatta.

After the Sothby's dinner Mrs. Coopersmith prevailed on us to donate the First Lady Tribute tablecloths to the State Department to be used at their various functions and dinner parties. At an afternoon tea in the State Department's diplomatic reception room Jim and I personally presented them to Clement Conger, the curator who had overseen Jackie Kennedy's restoration of the White House.

Individually or together, Jim and I were constantly in cars, planes, or trains, traveling the world to meetings and conventions. Jim had been elected to the board of the International Franchise Association, and subsequently became its chairman. The IFA trips, added to IDD's Grand Destination adventures, provided us with some extraordinary travel experiences. When customs agents inquired whether a trip was for business or pleasure, it was difficult to

respond. Those two aspects of Jim's and my life were so intertwined it was hard to tell them apart

Besides our annual conferences, we get together with our IDD associates as a group every other year for a Grand Destination trip. My memories and photo albums have grown to include scenes from the Costa del Sol, London, Rome, Capri, Venice, Paris , cruises to Alaska and the Greek isles, and most recently a Baltic cruise where one of our stops was St. Petersburg.

Clement Conger graciously accepting our gift of tablecloths made out of the First Lady's fabric for use at State Department affairs.

Of course, for me, the most rewarding trip was when I led a band of IDD interior decorators on my return to Paris in 1994. It was easy planning the itinerary for a group of people who shared my infatuation for the same things I had enjoyed as a student ten years earlier.

Their rapture doubled my pleasure revisiting the Louvre and Versailles; antiquing at the Marche Puce, the world's best known flea market; and shopping at the Galleries Lafayette and Printemps, two of the city's grand department stores. I arranged for our decorators to tour the rooms of precious furnishings and objet d'art at the Musee Des Arts Decoratifs with one of my professors from my Parson Design school days. And, I made sure they stayed at a five star hotel, the centrally located and luxuriously appointed Le Grand Intercontinental, adjacent to the Opera House and home of the Café de la Paix.

Over the years, in addition to the Presidential Suite at the Plaza Hotel for Donald Trump, IDD has had its share of noteworthy decorating assignments. One was the media room in the Show House for PBS's *This Old House*, another was decorating Robert Stern's American Dream House for *Life Magazine*. The challenge in both instances was merging new trends with classic furnishings, and designing fashionable looking rooms that would not appear dated in a couple of years. The media room for *This Old House* was a good example of pairing the latest technology with the best of traditional design. In reviewing the pictures of these two projects covered in my book, *Smart & Simple Decorating*, I am pleased to report that the decorating has met the test of time, beautifully.

The PBS showhouse was decorated by Anne Fawcett and her team from Massachusetts.

One of the most unforgettable events that Dec Den's PR Patti instigated was our involvement with the Frank Sinatra Celebrity Invitational Golf Tournament in Palm Springs. The tournament benefited the Barbara Sinatra Children's Center at The Eisenhower Medical Center and Desert Hospital. Our job was to create a stage set where Frank and Barbara Sinatra and some of their old friends would sit and be observed during the first couple of night's dinner ceremonies. A banner with Decorating Den's name was to be prominently displayed above the stage.

A perk of Dec Den's sponsorship was that Jim and three lucky franchisees and their husbands got to play golf with the celebrity guests, and of course participate in all of the social events. My husband had just recently taken up golf and I thought he had a lot of nerve teeing off in front of TV cameras with hundreds of people watching. Even if I considered myself a golfer, I would never have had the courage to hit the ball while all eyes were upon me. Yet when I accepted an invitation to be a speaker at the fashion show luncheon given by the wealthy doyennes of this desert community, I lined myself up for an equally intimidating set of circumstances.

A ladies' luncheon in Washington, D.C. is filled with women on noon breaks from their jobs. In Palm Springs the pampered ladies of leisure were just starting their day when they arrived in their Rollses, Bentleys and chauffeured limos. Their taut faces were framed in fashionably coiffed hairstyles, and their personally trained bodies were covered in tantalizing Escada ensembles, Chanel chains, and vivacious Versace. Their jewels were definitely not costume, and they were carrying the real, not the mock versions of Judith Leiber purses, Louis Vuitton satchels, and diamond quilted bags with intertwining "C's."

The Life Magazine *House was decorated by Terri Ervin and Judith Slaughter.*

Prior to facing this intimidating assembly of gorgeously groomed women, I wondered what I could do to bolster my confidence and distract their eyes away from my average outfit and baubles. The answer came to me in a nightmare . . . pull the old hat out of the box! I have found that a hat, the bigger the better, is the cheapest ticket to self-assurance and the best accessory for attracting attention.

To make matters even more daunting, when the day of the luncheon arrived, I followed a dozen willowy young women modeling outfits from Mondi, a presentation by a chic moderator from *Vogue* magazine, and the soigné chairman of the affair who represented the Palm Springs in-crowd. And like a soprano singing a cappella, I had to deliver my remarks exposed to the audience without the assistance of a podium to lean on. Merci dieu pour mon chapeau!

At the last event of the tournament, the Awards Banquet, we witnessed ole' blue eyes holding the audience in a spell as he crooned his signature lyrics at what would be the final performance of Frank Sinatra's life. Later when we arrived at the Sinatra's home for a farewell party, we found our hostess as relieved and relaxed as any non-celebrity woman would be at pulling off a successful charity affair.

As we celebrate forty years in the home furnishings business, the saga of Interiors by Decorating Den continues to unfold. We keep on adding to our roster of interior decorators, and work with an ever expanding list of clients who made the decision that when it came to decorating their homes they deserved ... the professional touch.

I used a hat and a smile to bolster my confidence when I addressed a ladies luncheon during the Frank Sinatra Celebrity Invitational Golf Tournament in Palm Springs.

Jim and I enjoying a moment
at a party in the home of Frank and
Barbara Sinatra.

Chapter 3

The Decorator's Decorator

It's my clients that make my business so personally rewarding and fun. Décor and design are a wonderful refuge in a harsh world, and a smile on my customer's face assures me that I have created a pleasing space for her.

— Sally Giar

Why It's So Hard to Decorate Your Own Home

Shortly after I made the announcement at IDD's 2007 conference in Nashville about writing a book focusing on "how to work with a professional," I received a note from **Sally Giar** with pictures of several rooms she was planning to enter in the next Dream Room contest. When I expressed an interest Sally sent me the following, compelling letter and irresistible picture of her clients.

The Corbett's family room designed by Sally Giar as a colorful living area for cozy evenings together.

Meet the Decorator

Dear Carol,

I want to share with you an interesting story about a client of mine. Her name is Cheryl Corbett. She called one day to schedule an appointment for window treatments in her master bedroom. We set an appointment; and while I was there, Cheryl shared with me that she had seen my ads for the past few years in the local newspaper, and that she knew one day she would call me to help her decorate her home. That afternoon, I left her home with a nice sale, and that was the beginning . . . .

Before we had even completed the bedroom, we started working on other areas of her home, going from choosing wallpaper, to window treatments, bedding, area rugs, lighting, furniture, and accessories. Cheryl was so easy to work with, and I really enjoyed her company, not to mention the dog, cat, bird, and rabbit that always seemed to be there in the middle of it all. It seemed that Cheryl and I were always on the same wavelength—she understood what I was trying to convey, and I knew what she was looking for.

The months went by and I knew her final big project would be the family room. With the holidays soon upon us, we got things started and picked paint colors, carpet, furniture, window treatments, lighting, accessories—all scheduled to be completed in January.

In mid December, after a nice lunch that I wanted to treat her to, Cheryl said she had something that she needed to share with me. She had wanted to tell me from the beginning, but was concerned it might interfere with our relationship. So now that everything was just about completed, she informed me that she has a degree in interior design. After I got over the shock, I was quite amused—everything made sense at that point. Although only in her forties, an illness had stopped her from working. She had seen my ads and decorating articles for quite some time, and knew that I would have the resources to decorate her lovely new home.

Clients Cheryl and Tom Corbett with Elmo the dog, Goony the cat, Benjamin the rabbit, and Spike the bird.

The day I talked to Cheryl Corbett she was waiting for Sally to deliver a few more items. "What I like best," she told me, "is not having to drag around on my own looking for things. I know what I like and don't like, but Sally did the footwork for me." Take a look at the results.

The Family Room

The write-up on Sally's Dream Room board explains the design she came up with to help Cheryl and Tom adjust to a move from a condo to a more spacious home in golf course community. Their desire was to change the boring and outdated family room into a colorful and cozy living area where they could spend evenings enjoying time together, along with their four animals. In particular, they were seeking ideas to disguise what Cheryl referred to as the "Titanic" look above the fireplace.

By covering the fireplace, entertainment center, and dry bar with honey-colored wood cabinetry and decorating the windows with faux wrought iron scrolls, Sally significantly enhanced the room's focal point. At the other windows, the decorator hung plaid drapery with attached fringed valances from iron poles. The bold persimmon color she chose for the walls reflects her clients' sunny, outgoing personalities.

An often-overlooked device for giving impact to a room is angling furniture the way Sally did, placing two new loveseats, covered in a dark rusty-red floral chenille, facing each other in the center of the room. Ottomans provide the optional use as cocktail tables, or additional seating. Sally combined new lamps, leopard pillows, and touches of black with the Corbett's personal collections and artifacts.

Inset: Corbett bedroom before.
Left: A new king-sized bed with upholstered
headboard graces this relaxing forest-green
master bedroom.

Master Bedroom

A king bed and generously sized chests were the first purchases Cheryl and Tom made after they moved. Sally added an upholstered headboard to the bed, now layered in an array of bronze and sienna textures. Painting the walls a relaxed shade of forest green converted the stark space into a soothing refuge.

When I spoke with Sally's client, I asked her if she used her beautiful tufted chaise which was angled in front of the windows. Cheryl confessed that she hadn't, but said that just looking at it made her feel relaxed. The corner windows are dressed with a silky swagged valance, hung from bronze medallions over contrasting floor length flaxen cascades. Tiffany-style lamps, intricate metal art, and an elaborate ceiling fan were Sally's finishing touches to this romantic retreat.

An inviting tufted chaise is relaxing just to look at.

Master Bath

As for the master bath, bronze was chosen as the featured color and finish. Along with antique bronze knobs, Sally affixed dramatic frames to the mirrors above his and her vanities. A chandelier decorated with shades and crystal drops, a fringed valance, and a plush floral area rug contribute further to the classic elegance the Corbett's desired.

Inset: The Corbett's tired looking master bath before.
Left: Fresh color and pattern and new window treatment and rug update the old bathroom.

The only thing atypical about this IDD project was that the client herself was an interior designer. Otherwise, the steps the decorator followed were the same; interviewing and listening to the client, discovering the client's desires and goals, coming up with a decorating plan and product options—and, best of all, handling all of the particulars entailed in completing a project.

Above: A bevy of beautiful accessories add to the charm of the revamped space.

If a man could mount to heaven and survey the mighty universe his admiration of its beauties would be much diminished unless he had someone to share in his pleasure.

— Miguel de Cervantes

Chapter 4

Marrying His and Her Personalities and Possessions

At the grand opening of her Jacques Renee Boutique, the flamboyant Flor Trujillo, the daughter of the former dictator of the Dominican Republic, went out of her way to introduce me to Jim Bugg, the franchisor of her new cosmetics business. Only a romantic like the multi-married Flor would have foreseen potential for the diplomat's daughter and the son of a dirt scrabble farmer. But in true love-conquers-all fashion, three months later this charmed encounter led to marriage.

Combining the Tastes of Two Strong Personalities Is a True Test of Love

I revel in reminiscing how unconcerned I was about the glaring impediments to our union: Kentucky country boy–New York City girl, Baptist-Catholic, divorced–never been married, five kids–no children. But after seeing his house, what worried me most was how to get our two extremely different households to live together happily ever after.

The stuffed African animal head trophies on the walls of Jim's Georgetown house did not disturb me as much as the shocking matador-cape-red wall-to-wall carpet that covered every square inch of his floors. I pride myself on being open-minded about other people's taste in decorating. I want to believe that there are no bad

After 40 years of marriage, I know well how to combine "hers" with "his" in lovely harmony.

colors, just wrong decisions on how to use them. But other than Jim, only *el toro* would have appreciated that much red.

Then there were the huge pair of elephant tusks framing the fireplace, and one of the animal's feet holding up a glass table top cut in the outline of the continent of Africa, which Jim informed me was also the shape of an elephant's ear. The bachelor *pièce de résistance*—a polar bear rug was sited in front of the fireplace under the aforementioned table. Adding to this unique decorating scheme were incongruous sheer Austrian shades he had inherited along with an indiscriminate selection of après-divorce furniture. And this was just the living room.

Once I resolved ways to marry my pale yellow sofa and ordinary furnishings with Jim's brilliant red carpet and unique accumulation of trophies and leftovers, I vowed to take him as my husband and his home as my new residence.

By the day we married, my pale yellow sofa, Barcelona cocktail table, and dramatic lamp were already wedded to Jim's red carpet, polar bear rug, and elephant tusks. Jim's Labrador retriever, Tiger.

Meet the Decorator

When it comes to decorating and marrying his and hers personalities and possessions into a cohesive whole, no one can do it better for you than a decorator—especially IDD designer **Tonie VanderHulst.** Not only for her clients, but in her own home and business life, she practices the art of respectful compromise in these delicate situations.

Eleven years ago Tonie's husband Pete left the corporate world to join her full-time in running her IDD franchise and managing a region. Tonie knew that to make a success of their partnership would require compromise, diplomacy, and love. When I asked her how she handled the inevitable disagreements, she offered a bit of practical advice, "Learn to resolve your differences without placing blame on each other. We just get over it." Another of Tonie's observations that Jim and I relate to is: "Sometimes working extreme hours is what it takes, but at least we get to be together doing what we love."

Romancing the Bedroom

Tonie and Pete VanderHulst are recent empty nesters who spend many hours away from home running their business. After working hard together on their clients' homes, they longed for their bedroom to be a romantic retreat where they could escape the world and enjoy each other's company. Tonie loves the color purple and her favorite city is Venice. Pete's main request was, "Spare me from too many florals."

Considering both her own and her husband's wishes, Tonie dressed the room in sumptuous silks and sheers, in purples and golds. To accentuate the 10-foot height of the room, she painted the ceilings aubergine and installed deeper crown molding. The walls are now covered in a beautiful damask paper that closely blends with the soft gold in the carpet, and the windows are draped in gold-and-purple-striped silk, embellished with fringe.

Tonie dressed her new iron bed with a luxurious comforter, pillows, and an elegant silk embroidered sheer loosely wrapped around the top railings. Remote control room-darkening Roman shades make it easy to sleep in on weekends. Tonie and Pete report that life in their child-empty home is filled with love and sweeter than ever.

Tonie and Pete VanderHulst are one of IDD's husband and wife franchise partnerships.

A love for Venice and the color purple inspired this romantic bedroom décor.

Inset: A luxurious tufted recamier captures the ambiance of Venice.

*A pair of overstuffed club chairs and an
ottoman were positioned for comfort and
conversation, and to enjoy the view of the
fireplace and outside the door.*

Weekend Getaway

Tracy Lafferty's clients are a husband and wife who work in two different states and rendezvous on weekends in yet another state. She helped them design a plan to extend the back of a 1920's bungalow style house and create a sublime master suite.

Warm colors and a blend of Mission style furniture with modern finishes and fabrics, were used by Tracy to give the space a contemporary feel, while honoring the era of the house. For her clients' extensive collection of books, she designed custom glass-enclosed bookcases and furniture. For complete seclusion when needed, suede Roman shades cover windows and doors. All week long husband and wife anticipate returning to their weekend retreat to enjoy their shared passions for reading, sipping fine wines, and simple quiet moments together.

*Autumnal colors
and Mission style
furniture suit the
getaway spirit
of this bungalow
house.*

*Inset: Suede Roman shades with attached
opaque ones allow for light and complete
seclusion when they are pulled down.*

43

The colors and elements of this home office were carefully selected to work for both husband and wife.

A comfortable wing chair provides the room with a cozy place for reading.

Home Office Partners

Husband and wife agreed on establishing a joint home office in a small square space off of the living room. Decorators **Barbara Elliott** and her sister **Jennifer Ward-Woods** knew that this important space had to reflect the grand style of the rest of the home, as well as establish an environment that would appeal to both sexes.

The decorators' choice of a faux leather finish for the walls and embroidered sheers was one way of satisfying his and her tastes. Another was selecting a desk chair that adjusts to meet the height requirements of either husband or wife. The wood desk, high wingback chair, wool rug, and bronze chandelier are simply beautiful and defy gender labels. Adding a bit of extra interest to the clients' personal collection of books and photos are a few well-chosen new accessories.

*When it came to color and mood, the
decorator was thoughtful in including the
individual preferences of the homeowners.*

Spouse Friendly

Before they launched into updating their new home, this couple found themselves overwhelmed by the size of their great room. Adding to the dilemma was the wife's preference for rich and upscale furnishings, while her husband wanted the finished look to be masculine and durable.

The solution was that each time their decorator **Dolores Baker** introduced something that appealed to his taste–such as the leather sectional–she balanced the room with feminine touches. For the wife it was an overstuffed chair and ottoman. When it came to the vast expanse of windows, Delores designed a treatment that combined faux suede flip scarves with silky embroidered drapery and playful tassels. Using brown-tinted neutrals, rusty red, and an Oriental style rug, she brought harmony not only to the look of the room, but to the couple as well.

Designed around the handsome Bob Mackie
bed, this bedroom favors the Safari interests
of both husband and wife.

Targeting Drama

For her big-game hunting husband and wife clients, decorator **Joyce Means** selected the impressive leather sleigh bed designed by Bob Mackie to warm up and play down the overpowering scale of this master bedroom. She layered the bed with an assortment of luscious patterned fabrics in tones of burgundy, green, and cream. To appeal to their hunting spirits, Joyce added a punch of zebra fabric along the edge of the comforter and the Euro-size pillows, complementing the natural zebra skin rug on the floor.

Walls have been textured and faux-painted in warm tones, and for the windows Joyce designed tassel-trimmed valances to be board-mounted over stationary drapery panels. Underneath these panels are motorized cellular shade treatments to give privacy when needed without obstructing the magnificent view. Above the headboard, a large piece of artwork makes a statement and balances the height of the wall. The clients are enamored with the look and feel of their new décor.

...the professional touch

Along with their understanding of the masculine and feminine, the yin and yang of design, interior decorators have the invaluable skill to mediate the individual opinions and tastes of husbands and wives and bring the wishes of each into a room both can enjoy.

The real voyage of discovery consists not in seeing new landscapes but in seeing with new eyes.

— Marcel Proust

Chapter 5

Decorating Is A Work In Progress

Debunking the Myth that One Must Start from Scratch

One of the prime obstacles that prevent people from consulting with an interior decorator is the fear they will have to start from scratch. Let me put that myth to rest—decorating, like life, is an ongoing and evolving work in progress. When the time comes to revive the tired rooms in your home, a decorator can offer invaluable assistance in devising a plan around the things you want to keep, and at the same time, take into account your ever-emerging status and lifestyle.

There is no better motivation for rejuvenating the interior of a home than knowing company is coming, especially if your guests will be interior decorators. Every year during IDD's conference we honor a select group of our franchise owners at the Chairman's Circle dinner. This time, due to the close proximity of the convention site to where Jim and I live, the plans included a champagne reception at our home prior to the celebratory dinner.

In anticipation of opening up my home to the discerning eyes of professionals, which was to be followed days later by a photo shoot for this book, I began analyzing each room. While I have always considered decorating my residence an evolving work-in-progress not predicated on trends, I felt foolish admitting that over a decade had passed since any serious updates had been done to the living room.

My style of decorating is mixing the old (the armoire) with the new (the chaise lounge).

It was not that the dark draperies and rug were in bad condition or no longer attractive, I simply had tired of the busy patterns and black and coral color scheme. I also concluded that the space was overcrowded with large pieces of upholstered furniture, and that the time had come to forego my attachment to the old pewter cocktail table. The heavy walnut armoire was given a new position of prominence. The wallpaper has been up longer than I care to admit, but its subtle, toasty wood color became more relevant when paired with the new iridescent aqua faux silk drapery panels. My sofa was

also a keeper, but with a pale aqua chenille slipcover and a single seat cushion the look was totally changed.

The two wood-framed chairs, chaise, cocktail table, and étagère are new; but it is my new area rug that deserves the credit for making the most impact on the room's revived look. When I designed model homes for builders, I had no problem making selections; but I labor endlessly over each decision when I am decorating for myself. The exception was the day I walked into a showroom and described to the manager that I was looking for something along the lines of a

Simply changing to a soothing green color palette made the biggest difference towards the new look of the living room.

Here we see Jim minutes before the photographer arrived applying his latest touchup to the Labrador Retriever painting in our living room.

needlepoint rug in the style and colors of famed French decorator, the late Madeleine Castaing.

Sometimes the picture is so clear in my mind that I have difficulty describing what I want, but the savvy showroom manager understood perfectly. From the time he showed me a possible option, to my hesitating for a moment because it seemed too perfect to be true, to making the purchase, was, according to him, the fastest sale he ever made.

While I had managed to get my house decorated in time for the party and subsequently for the photo shoot, my living room continues to be a work in progress. Ten minutes before photographer Gordon Beall set up his camera equipment, my husband was making his latest change to the dog portrait that hangs over the sofa in our living room. This is a sporadic activity that has been going on for so many years that I hardly take notice anymore.

Meet the Decorator

Terri Ervin and her husband **Allen Hugo** joined Decorating Den a few months after Jim and I did. It hardly seems possible that sons Matt and Zach, whose rooms were featured in my second book *Divine Design*, now have apartments of their own. What I have always admired about Terri is that no matter how beautiful she made her home, not one room was off limits to her sons. Raising two active boys no doubt increased Terri's awareness of how balancing panache with just the right amount of practicality is important in most households.

Changing Lifestyles

The decorating of Terri's home continues as she accommodates her current lifestyle and anticipates changes in the future. Terri is in the process of converting the upstairs bedrooms into a guest suite. In preparation for enjoying their senior years and staying away from stairs, even though I think that time is a long way off, she and Allen have moved into the former first floor guest room. I am familiar with this space since Jim and I have had the pleasure of staying there on several occasions.

Terri's plan was to give the room a whole new look while working around the existing wallcovering. The brown in the toile she selected pulls out the tones in the existing paper. Terri covered the bed with a pale blue quilt and added coordinating pillows and a contrasting throw. Her collection of brown and white plates that previously hung in the kitchen, now look perfectly at home displayed over the brass bed. New bamboo shades at the window also accentuate the brown in the fabric, and for a touch of typical Terri whimsy, she skirted a night table in a fun animal print.

IDD Regional Directors Terri Ervin and Allen Hugo with their sons, Matt and Zach, around the age when their rooms, decorated by Mom, were featured in Divine Design.

Terri changed the colors and feeling of their former first floor guest room and turned it into a master bedroom.

Starting from Scratch

There are two ways to bring life back to expired rooms—working around existing furnishings or starting from scratch when the first option is no longer viable. "Clear out the old and create a bright and uplifting ambiance for my family room and dining room," was the plea of a single mother with a teenage daughter. One of the concerns she expressed to her decorator **Gloria Hill** was the intense light and heat that prevented her from opening the window shades during the day.

Before

In the dining room, Gloria used a console table as a sideboard, and added upholstered host chairs to spice up the wood table and side chairs.

In the family room, new furniture in a different arrangement, and the elevation of the big-screen TV to over the fireplace, gives the space a larger appearance and better traffic flow. For the dining room, Gloria added the softening element of upholstered host chairs, and visually opened the space by using a console table instead of a sideboard. With warm neutral tones Gloria established a sophisticated color palette that flows through both rooms. She addressed the sunlight issue by hanging blackout lined "eco-friendly" grass cloth woven shades over the UV treated windowpanes. On the strictly fashionable side, she chose two different but coordinating styles of drapery panels for each room.

Before

The whimsical bathroom.

Working Around

A pretty English garden print was decorator **Heidi Sowatsky's** starting point to changing this dowdy guest bedroom into the elegant Caribbean resort atmosphere. The floral pattern maintains the traditional look, but the lime-green-and-rosy-pink on a sea of Caribbean blue contribute to the room's fresh appeal. To maintain the light and airy feel and contrast with the dark wood, the decorator covered her client's classic four-poster bed in white matelasse. It is actually a duvet cover that can be filled with a down insert for chilly northern nights. Floral pillow shams and dust ruffle complete the ensemble. While the ceiling fan and heliconia plant supply breezy tropical touches, a *giclée* portrait of a Cavalier King Spaniel furthers the room's British origins.

*Inset: New contemporary iron table, chairs,
and chandelier brighten the area.*

Shelley Rodner's client wanted a kitchen update without making any major structural changes—in other words, work around the existing cabinets. The one exception was removing the bank of ceiling-mounted cabinets between the kitchen and breakfast areas, which instantly opened up the space and the view to the bay window. The old wallpaper was removed, and the countertops were replaced with granite that paired nicely with the dramatic new black backsplash. She had the existing cabinets stripped and repainted, changed the hardware, and added crown molding. The knee wall separating the family room from the breakfast space was reinvented with the same black granite that was used for the backsplash.

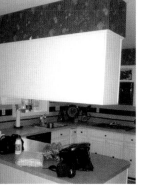

*Removing the bank of ceiling mounted
cabinets opened up the space and the view.*

This was the first room people saw upon entering the home of **Jeanne Grier's** clients. They were content with their off-white sofa, pair of upholstered armchairs, tables and mirror, but wanted Jeanne to complete the space and add some *pizzazz*. An area rug that includes shades of rusty red and basil green, as well as cream on a black background was the starting point.

Building on this color combination, Jeanne selected a brown-and-black check taffeta for the tassel tied-back drapery panels, which draw attention to the 9-foot ceilings and the ornate mirror. A new armchair upholstered in stripes of black and gold further repeats the new color scheme. Instead of traditional art above the fireplace and for a more personal and modern touch, Jeanne framed black-and-white photos of her client's favorite places in Italy.

Color and fabric turned a bland space into a sophisticated dining room.

Before

To make her clients' dining room come alive, decorator **Beverly Barrett** worked her magic with color and fabric. The chocolate brown she selected for the walls and tray ceiling provide a striking contrast against the surviving lightly stained furniture. At the window, she installed simple, yet impacting drapery panels on rods with contemporary spiral finials, and new honeycomb shades that blend with the darker walls. Chair seats were brought up-to-date with a brown geometric fabric. A centerpiece of berry stems and glass holders supply a final touch of glimmer to the look of the space.

Chapter 6

Living Well Is
All about Family and Friends

*M*ention family and friends and I risk sounding like a sentimental fool, confessing that I deeply love my accidental acquisitions . . . the Buggs and Dec Den. Without getting too sappy, let it suffice for me to say that my existence would have been a lot duller and drearier without them. It's also true that over the past quarter of a century the intertwining of my personal life with my business life has morphed friends into family, and vice versa. In the beginning, I imagined franchisees would strictly be business associates, but I never could have predicted the way these women would become my buddies, chums, and pals. Let me tell you the evolving story of one of these friendships.

Decorator Lauren Riddiough has created a family room where comfort and fashion blend beautifully and guests are always welcome.

Meet the Decorator

While my husband was investigating Decorating Den, he attended an orientation program where he met Linda Riddiough and her husband Mick. Although obviously enthusiastic about the potential of the franchise, Jim was equally excited about meeting this young woman. "Carol, if we get involved with Decorating Den I have found the perfect person for your region,"

he told me. We did get involved, and Linda did indeed turn out to be one of my first franchisees. Beyond her interest in interior decorating, Linda's other passion was her family, husband Mick and their two-year-old daughter Lauren.

Those first few years, Linda and I laughed (a sense of humor is a prerequisite for being an interior decorator) about the various challenges I encountered establishing the region and Linda starting up her franchise. Linda was my sidekick when I worked on the Dream Room Contest or toured the High Point Furniture Market.

Only one thing diverted Linda's attention away from Dec Den business and that was her adorable daughter. Linda went so far as to give up her sporty convertible for a bigger vehicle with a trailer so she could haul Lauren's horse to equestrian competitions; and over time Lauren was awarded enough championship blue ribbons to cover the walls of her bedroom. There was more parental pride for Lauren when she graduated from college with a degree in psychology, achieving the first step in her goal of being a sports psychologist.

Lauren had been accepted at the Citadel and was ready to begin work on her masters degree when Linda and Mick got a call from their daughter informing them, "I do not think this is what I really want to do after all." Linda told me how shocked they were at Lauren's change of heart, since being a psychologist was all she had ever talked about. When they asked her what her plan was, she asked, "How would you feel about my owning an Interiors by Decorating Den franchise?" Disbelieving what she was hearing, Linda asked her daughter how come she had never mentioned this before. Lauren replied, "I've been thinking about it for a long time. Mom, don't you think I watched you all of those years when you had a franchise!"

Now Linda is reliving her early Dec Den days as she watches Lauren start her franchise and grow as a business woman, "She is a real system follower," my old friend proudly confided. "Lauren proves everyday that the IDD system works."

Linda also enjoyed telling me that in addition to Lauren's taking advantage of IDD's newer marketing strategies, her daughter also hand delivers flyers to promote her business. I laughed when Linda relayed how she used to drive the van around her target neighborhood and Mick would hold two-year-old Lauren out the window so she could put flyers in the boxes. Some good ideas never die.

Linda recently wrote me another chapter in this story. She joined her daughter on a photo shoot where the photographer was Gordon Beall, a flash from our past. She reminded Gordon, "Twenty-four years ago I was helping Carol Bugg when you shot the rooms in her home for her first book." (I am pleased to report that it was Gordon who photographed my newly revamped rooms and the cover of this book.)

Life is all about family and friends and the way even if you do not see each other often, or contact is limited to e-mails, when you do get together there is that pleasant familiarity of easily picking up where you left off. Linda, who still works in marketing for IDD, and I now have an added bond in the newest interior decorator **Lauren Riddiough**.

Making Everyday Rooms Warm and Welcoming for Guests Too

Of all the requests we hear from clients, their most frequently asked is to make warm and welcoming the rooms where they entertain friends and family. And when it came to decorating the family room in their new home that is exactly what Lauren's new client asked for in their very first directive: "Turn the prominent area that everyone sees as they enter the home into a pleasant space for entertaining." But equally important was making the family room comfortable enough to accommodate their everyday lifestyle, which included an 11-month-old daughter.

Lauren had the room painted a neutral color, except for the focal point fireplace wall, where she opted for a rich shade of red. The custom faux iron "T", which represents the family name, accents the height of the stone facade and ties in with the other wrought iron elements in the room. For easy maintenance, Lauren's selection of a soft olefin fiber-based rug was the perfect choice for entertaining, whether children or adults. Defining the open floor plan are a sofa, *bergère* (upholstered French arm chair) and ottoman, and two chairs that she positioned to take full advantage of their fabulous "X" backs. These comfortable upholstered pieces, along with the deep wood tones, tailored chocolate draperies, and mix of gorgeous textures make this the most-used room in Lauren's clients' home.

*Most days it is only my husband and I
enjoying breakfast or lunch at the newly
skirted table in front of the window.*

My Dining Room

While far less demanding than updating my living room, a dining room spruce-up was also in order before my photo shoot. This room is saturated with memories of numerous birthday and holiday celebrations, one wedding reception, a christening luncheon, a rehearsal dinner, two college reunions, and meals enjoyed daily by a party of two at a petite version of our main Country French dining table. Adding to the room's allure is the vivid recollection I have of the circumstance surrounding the accumulation of each Louis XV furnishing and Labrador retriever object.

My antiques, a *panetiere* (French breadbox) and *Mobilier repoussé* pendulum clock, were well worth the dent they made in my savings account; and with thirty years added to the time when I purchased the dining tables, they now qualify as antiques. The chairs, breakfront, chandelier, and duck press are reproduction Louis XV, but that does not make them any less valuable to me. The considerate gifts from family and friends constitute the foundation for my assemblage of Labrador baubles and books.

Both of the tables have self-contained leaves that adapt to intimate settings for dinner parties, or cocktail buffets, or with the extensions lifted in place we can seat fifteen for family gatherings.

I have finally satisfied my long harbored desire to fully upholster the Louis XV style chairs in green velvet with a check for the back. One item yet to be fully realized is the rug, but for right now the inexpensive green-banded sisal rug works well with the color changes. That part of the dining room decorating story, like some other things in my home, is to be continued.

*I take as much pleasure in my reproduction
Louis XV furnishings as I do the few
antiques.*

An antique panetiere *(French breadbox)
hangs over a chest that holds my linens.*

On the other side of the basement, stools surround the custom bar in front of the wine cellar and the adjacent high-top table.

Fun and Games in the Basement

Another space decorated with entertaining in mind was this former empty basement. First on decorator **Suzanne Price's** agenda was coming up with an effective floor plan to ensure comfort and flow for large crowds. Her design called for the space to be divided into thirds to accommodate three distinct functions.

Suzanne's astute furniture arranging and choice of earthy tones warmed up an impossibly large cold space, making it a most inviting space to share with others.

An adjustable game table can be raised for a game of cards or transformed to coffee table height, while club chairs on casters provide ultimate flexibility. A round braided rug that picks up the room's earthy tones adds to the coziness of this area of the basement.

An olive green shag rug, a chenille-covered sectional sofa, and a leather recliner define the television viewing area.

The goal for this extra room off of the family room was to turn it into a music lounge as an overflow space for entertaining.

Music Lounge

Lisa Landry began her design of this music lounge with a funky but comfortable daybed between the windows, a perfect place for lounging and playing the guitar. The addition of oversized cushions allows guests to spread them around the floor. Displaying a few guitars on the wall identifies the purpose of the room and provides instruments for guests to play. Retro lamps supply mood lighting, which is reflected in the oversized floor mirror on wheels, enlarging the not-so-big space. Finishing out the room with graphic, music-related wall art, movable nesting tables, and extra chairs, Lisa created a flexible, easy-going space that is everchanging.

Since the client's daughter is a musician, the family spends a lot of time hanging out as a group and with friends, playing and listening to music.

Le Cinema de Bijou

For their dream setting, **Lisa Landry** and her clients decided to recreate the look of an old-style, Hollywood-inspired movie theatre. For the all-important first impression, guests enter by walking past a green velvet rope, then passing through luxurious gold pulled-back draperies. Above their heads is a plaque reading, "Le Cinema de Bijou," translated, "a small delicate jewel of a theatre," a reference to the client's love of Paris. No movie theatre would be complete without drinks and popcorn.

In the main theatre, wall sconces and dramatically lit gilt framed posters add ambiance. For the seating, decorator and clients agreed upon classic black leather recliners, which will take a beating and never go out of style. To frame the drop-down screen, and help with sound absorption, Lisa designed an ornate drapery treatment of brocaded velvet. Lisa, who never misses a detail, provided a box of tissues for those inevitable tear-jerker flicks.

*No tickets are required to enter this theatre,
only an invitation from the homeowners.*

Returning Child/Guest Room

Beauty being in the age and eye of the beholder, a guest room should appeal to men and women, a variety of tastes, and be appropriate for both dear friends and returning children. Take, for example, how IDD sister partners **Barbara Elliott** and **Jennifer Ward-Woods** tackled the challenges of a small space that in addition to overnight visitors would be home to their client's daughter when on school breaks and in the summer. The end result is a desirable retreat whether you are a junior or a senior, male or female.

Their design is a study in gender friendly decorating; a mix of lush and tailored details, bold and soft color contrasts. The decorators' decision to paint the walls with three horizontal stripes in different shades of green, separated by two-inch bands supplied the room with instant verve. In contrast to the olive, sage, and mint scheme they selected black furniture; a sleek comfortable queen size leather sleigh bed, and a tall chest and night stand that offer plenty of drawer space.

At the windows they veered towards the feminine with luxurious tufted button silk panels, and for the bedding went for a more streamlined tailored look, but accessorized with a bevy of gorgeous pillows. The tall iron-trimmed, floor-length mirror was not only a practical consideration, but also one that served to open up the room and reflect the light. Another visually expansive decision was to leave the legs of the bed and the chaise unskirted and exposed. This way more of the mock zebra rug, placed on a jaunty angle is visible. As a final touch, they hung a series of porcelain wall discs on the side wall–an expression of the multiple personalities of their client's most reliable guest, their college student daughter.

Thanksgiving Table

There is nothing more pleasurable than getting together with family and friends in a home that is decorated in all its glory for holiday celebrations. A delight in any season, the rich warm coral red, a favorite of **Becky Shearn's** client, is especially appropriate for festive gatherings. Here we see how Becky helped her client get the dining room ready to welcome home the family for a wonderful Thanksgiving dinner.

The bay window view from across the table.

Holiday Entertaining

Lack of eating space in the kitchen resulted in this dining room being used on a daily basis. Decorator **Luella Smith's** challenge was to take the woefully out-of-date space and convert it into a dining room that would be pretty enough for holiday decorating and entertaining, yet durable enough for the whole family–which included two young, athletic boys.

Luella chose a palette of bold reds and mustard yellow to reflect the fun-loving, vibrant personality of her client. Yellow floral drapery panels are contrasted against ruby red tone-on-tone striped walls. For privacy as well as sun protection, she added roller shades with a decorative edge. The existing chairs were reupholstered in a durable, subtle red plaid. Completing the transformation are a new chandelier and beautiful botanical prints for the walls. Christmas in this home is all about family, friends, and food as the table takes center stage in this updated room.

*The window treatments in my library
were made both to keep out the cold
and beautify the windows.*

Chapter 7

Designing Windows

*B*ecause of the immediate need for privacy, covering a window is usually the first decorating element addressed in a new house, but it is also rare that someone who moves into an older home wants to keep the existing draperies. People might try to live with the previous owner's choice, but not for long.

Nowhere is finding the right balance of aesthetics and function more important and difficult to achieve than in creating window treatments. Considering the steps required—designing, measuring, fabricating and installing—it amazes me that non-professionals would try to attempt it on their own.

Why It's Smart to Leave the Dressing of Windows to the Pros

There were two aspects of owning my own model home decorating business—both relating to numbers—that I tended to delay as long as possible. One was getting my figures ready for quarterly tax reports, and the other was preparing work orders for window treatments. When I was left with a choice, I tackled payables, receivables, and bottom lines before attacking drapery widths, lengths, and returns. To me, the consequences of making a mistake on my tax return were not as scary as putting down the incorrect measurements on a drapery work order.

Three decades ago there was no such thing as drapery puddling (allowing fabric to drape on floor); panel lengths had to be exact. To make matters worse, I was taking the measurements for dozens of windows off of the builder's blueprints. I was smart enough to realize early on that I needed the assurance (Help!) of the professionals in double-checking my figures, both in my business accounting and drapery measuring.

The Windows in My Library

My personal taste in window treatments is for simple panels hung on rods, you might even say it is my signature look. The one exception is the superbly crafted treatments that grace our library.

Unlike people who live in new homes and worry about the stagnant air from their windows being too tight and insulated, we face the opposite situation in our 90-year-old house. Rather than replace the original French windows, we opted to live with a little extra fresh air, or as in the case of the library, the interlined English chintz and a brilliant Scottish fabricator were the combination to blocking out cold weather conditions.

At that time Decorating Den had an office in the United Kingdom run by Sandy Campbell who was a pro at fabricating draperies with heavy interlinings suited to protect drafty old windows found in European homes. Sandy had been in our home and was familiar with the library windows.

On a trip to Scotland Sandy and I collaborated on the traverse drapery and inset cornice design, and finalized the details based on my measurements. Adding to the serendipity of this story was the way I literally stumbled across a basket in Sandy's workroom that just happened to contain the bouillon fringe (long twisted lengths of rope) that added the final panache to the cornice design.

Months later when the treatment finally arrived from Scotland, I was relieved to find what a perfect fit the panels and cornices were when George came to install them. (More of this story can be found in the chapter 9 on Art Appreciation)

Drapery Considerations

... the professional touch

Decorators start with the selection of drapery fabrics to coordinate with the colors and style in the room. Next comes an understanding of the vast selection of hard window products on the market, and deciding which one will best solve the concerns about privacy, light, and security. Making these product choices alone stymies most people, but those are nothing compared to measuring and ordering all of the components that go into dressing a single window. Consider these: pattern repeats, fullness, length, width, returns, linings, headings, trims, rods, rings, finials, holdbacks, and brackets. When it comes to blinds, shades, or shutters the questions are: inside/outside mounts, left-side/right-side cords, and the list continues. And then there is the installation.

There are times to save money, and there are times when doing so is foolish and not cost effective. I equate the difference between using a true professional drapery installer or leaving it to a handyman, with the results of using a professional photographer over taking an amateur snapshot. I believe in both instances it comes down to the equipment, or the tools of the trade, and the expert's knowledge of how to use them.

While Interiors by Decorating Den is happy to cover customers' windows with plain and simple treatments if that is what the situation calls for, we are known in the industry for our unique, intricate, elaborate window designs. On each project our interior decorators challenge themselves to come up with the most suitable and stunning design to fit the client's individual circumstances.

There are formulas to follow, but when it comes to figuring visually pleasing scale and proportion for graceful swags, the uncanny eye of the designer is an invaluable tool. In this chapter the focus is on some of our designers' most unusual situations and remarkable solutions, opening with a selection of complex designs created by the dynamic sister team of **Barbara Elliott** and **Jennifer Ward-Woods**.

Meet the Decorators

It was **Jennifer Ward-Wood**s who first came to my attention while she was working as a decorator for one of our franchise owners. She was so successful in rapidly acquiring a vast clientele that the following year Dec Den conference organizers invited her to be a speaker on a business success panel. A young lady in the audience who was looking for a silver bullet tip asked Jennifer to what she credited her success. I'll never forget her response: "I attribute it to a four letter word," she cunningly replied, pausing for 30 seconds before spelling, "W-O-R-K."

A short time later sister **Barbara Elliott** bought a franchise in a different state and asked Jennifer to join her. Now they run one of the most successful businesses in the company, and the best part is that these sisters love "W-O-R-K-ing" together.

Barbara Elliott and
Jennifer Ward-Woods,

Barbara Elliott and Jennifer Ward-Woods,
master designers of elaborate window
treatments, graciously complimenting me
on the simple drapery panels in my living
room.

Left: One of Barbara and Jennifer's elegant window creations.

Tall windows or average height, elaborate treatments, or tailored panels, each of Barbara and Jennifer's designs suit their client's individual situations.

The decorators' intention of draping the main window in this small living room (left) in a graceful halter design was to add drama, while leaving the molding around the windows exposed. Long swags were centered on a fluted rod, crisscrossed in couture fashion, and mounted on each side of the window with panels that flow to the floor. For light control, blinds and a layer of shimmering sheers were installed beneath the fluid swags.

Left: The design for this room's arched windows was doubly difficult since they are not the same size, nor are the spaces between them equal. The decorator's solution was to mask the window situation by making the arch lines coordinate with each other, rather than follow each individual arch. Three graceful silky iridescent blue/brown valances hang from burnished bronze medallions with matching flowing panels to the sides. Textured champagne sheer draperies under the valances can be drawn open by the client when she desires to let in the light and see the view.

Above: One of the features of this pretty dining room is the exquisite chocolate silk drapery with eight inch headings of diamond smocking, embellished with over 120 tiny covered buttons in contrasting aqua silk. The tab tops of the extra-full panels are gathered with bands in the color of the buttons, and individually hung from gilt rods with crackle blue finials.

Right: A double set of challenges facing the designer of this window treatment were the tight space for installation and the need for the new French doors to function easily. Her solutions were a stationary Duponi silk panel that could be tied back over the non-functioning door, and custom knife-pleated cornices that were flush mounted with the cabinetry. She added the luxurious details of lining and interlining the drapery and cornices, and embellishing the panels with beaded tassel fringe.

Ali Maricle's *unique square cornice boxes (left) turn these simple draped panels of fabric into an efficient way to allow easy access to the doors.*

In order to draw the eye up above the windows and follow the ceiling line, **Cheryl Smith** *angled solid silk drapery panels over angled stationary Roman shades. Medallions add interest to the top of the panels.*

If ever dressing a window required the skill of a professional, it was the wide and high expanse of glass in this living room designed by **Kris Miller**.

Drapery panels with a grommet heading suit the room's masculine décor for **Brenda Pinkus'** *husband's office.*

Kris Miller's clients were after a treatment that would reflect the grandeur of the space, without blocking the view. They also asked to incorporate a pair of decorative glass lanterns into the design. Keeping those prerequisites in mind, the decorator devised an impressive composition of swags and jabots in soft, washed chenille for draping the windows. She left two pockets of wall space for the client's Darni lanterns, aligning them with the highest drapery rod to create a continuation of the overall window treatment design. Inside mounted feather-light Silhouettes were a discreet yet functional choice for sun

control. Substantial carved drapery hardware and jeweled key tassels contribute additional drama to the opulent design.

Brenda Pinkus' window treatment for a husband's home office (above right) grandly brings attention to the height of the ceiling and the view out the window. On one long pole she mounted tricolor faux suede panels through grommets at the top of the window frames and between the windows to accentuate the height and give the illusion of one very large window. The lower panels were covered in roller shades for privacy without totally blocking out the light.

When presented with a huge master bedroom with four sets of windows, French sliders, and a curved bay, **Susan Owens'** idea was to maintain a cohesive look with the same fabric, but break it up with two different treatments. The fabric for all of the panels is a black sheer, embroidered with a gold scroll design that creates a striped effect. Susan backed it with a black blackout fabric so that only enough light can come through to allow the embroidered design to show up nicely.

In the bedroom area, she placed carved wood swag holders that project the draperies out far enough to clear the motorized shades behind them. The black fabric simply slips through the holders, puddling onto the floor for a casual romantic look. Behind the panels are soft folded blackout lined Roman shades made of French vanilla silk. For the bay area, Susan created traversing draperies on a track hidden inside the soffit and motorized for ease of operation.

This elaborate window treatment met the clients' desire for drama, romance, and casual elegance, as well as their need for complete blackout coverage for those times when they wanted to sleep in.

Decorators **Nola Shivers** and **Diane Barber** did not allow three awkwardly placed small clerestory windows to interfere with the placement of the four-poster bed on the only suitable wall in this bedroom. Instead they came up with a way to integrate them into the design and accentuate the bed itself. Their solution was to frame both the bed and the windows with extravagant silk swags and panels punctuated with button tufted cornice boxes that coordinate with the custom bedding. To further enhance the setting, decorative iron inserts were installed over the plain windows.

One of the room's many interesting designer details is the crystal bead encrusted chandelier hanging above the bed that helps accentuate the luminous quality of the chocolate faux finish on the ceiling and the deep golden rubbed crown molding. By embracing the difficulties of a challenging situation and coming up with unique solutions Nola and Diane designed a bedroom better than their clients had anticipated, a room and window treatments defined by...the professional touch.

A fundamental truth: man needs color.
Color is the immediate, spontaneous
expression of life.   — Le Corbusier

Chapter 8
The Charm of Color

Let the Experts Relieve
Your Anxiety over Color

Of all the elements in interior decorating, color attracts the most fervor and elicits the strongest opinions. Consideration about which color holds the most allure is like beauty, it's all in the eye of the beholder. There are no bad colors, just wrong decisions about using them. With those premises in mind, let's explore the magical power color had in changing the humdrum lives of some dull rooms.

From their positive reaction to the bold contemporary art in her studio, **Kathy Machir** surmised her new clients were ready to break away from tradition. After many years of living in a large home, they were making a significant lifestyle change and moving to a small standard track house located on a golf course. An adjustment to colors and furnishings was in order as well.

Painting the walls a vibrant color named "Wild Grass Root," with white satin crown molding emphasizing the intensity of the green, unified the long narrow rectangular living and dining areas. To soften the affect of the harsh desert sun, while also offering a soothing measure of privacy, Kathy installed scalloped valances and soft shades at the windows.

For the dining room Kathy designed a custom buffet with lighted cabinets to handle storage and a place for her clients to display their china and glassware. An oversized pom-pom rug supplies "eye-popping" definition to the area, and colorful mini-tassels add a flirty edge to the chairs of the new dining set.

Before

Left: A vibrant green revitalized the dining room and life of these down-sized homeowners.

Zest For Life

In the living room Kathy covered her client's old sofa in a vanilla fabric trimmed with bright cording, and with a sassy green and turquoise print she reinvigorated two favorite chairs. An introduction of contemporary art completes the look, which has given Kathy's clients a renewed zest for life that continues to astound their friends.

Before

Two Louis XVI oval back chairs covered in a tiger print, an elegant black granite top table, and a star-shaped red chenille ottoman fill out the seating arrangement. A collection of spheres is now prominently displayed on a gracefully skirted table. The new décor reflects Barbara Elliott's sojourns to Africa.

From Bland to Brilliant

When it came to reviving her own living room **Barbara Elliott** took a daring approach that only an experienced decorator would try. With the help of her sister Jennifer, she came up with a vibrant purple and red color scheme and an eclectic selection of furnishings. A favorite piece of artwork took on new importance once the walls were painted royal purple. For the transitional style sofa they chose a red texture with a subtle pattern. Simple cream silk pinch-pleated draperies with attached fringed valances were the choice for the windows.

Before

An Exuberant Color Combination

Room colors to complement the original artwork turned bland into beautiful, while a new furniture arrangement in this room de-emphasized the narrowness of the floor plan. **Myriam Payne** played gold walls against brilliant red and brassy tones. Two woven lounge chairs and a coffee table with rounded lines soften the design and add a distinct tropical atmosphere. By moving the sofa away from the main wall and floating the chairs opposite to it, the room appears to have wider proportions. Natural woven blinds and drapery panels in a harlequin pattern add to the living room's vibrant new look.

Before

Revamping A Beloved Home

Watching the homes in their 1960's neighborhood being remodeled and/or torn down, these clients came to the conclusion that the best approach to updating their house was for decorator **Virginia Smith** to work around the existing floor plan and to help them choose the right paint color to feature their art collection. The idea was to bring some new verve to the living and dining rooms for both adult entertaining and a retreat for teenagers.

Before

In the dining area a large focal point buffet provides storage and visual interest. The room is now ready for a casual lunch or to be dressed up for a formal affair.

The dark teal green that Virginia selected for the walls launched the metamorphosis. An old china cabinet was moved to the living room, establishing two distinct seating areas there with smaller scale furniture.

A settee and rattan chairs placed on an angle helped eliminate the "shotgun" effect down the middle of the room. New plank wood floors and Jacobean print drapery bring continuity to the dining and living room décor.

Fun and Funky Blues

Before **Karen Coleman** made any selections for this girl's room, she spent time interviewing the homeowner and her daughter about color, style, likes and dislikes. This led to a fun, funky, and fashionable circle design for drapery panels and bedspread, in our young client's favorite blues. Karen commissioned an artist to take his inspiration from the fabric and he covered the walls in circles. To soften the light at the window, Karen chose an electric lime green fuzzy sheer and repeated it in the dust ruffle and pillows. Functional and decorative grommets carry out the circle theme. "WOW" is everybody's response to this effervescent room.

This profound makeover is an example of one of Dec Den's commercial projects—revitalizing an office lobby area.

... the professional touch

Getting the colors right is one of a decorator's major contributions to matching a client's vision.

Interiors by Decorating Den's primary business is residential design. But our designers are called on for commercial projects as well. We are often hired to decorate restaurants, hotels, shops, and senior living facilities; but when it comes to commercial jobs, revitalizing office space is our most common undertaking.

A good example was the request by the owner of a prominent CPA firm in the Washington D.C. area for an update of his reception and office areas. He told **Ellen Fernandez** he wanted clean contemporary lines, a space that did not feel cold and commercial, and that he envisioned something spectacular for the hallway. He also explained that the design had to satisfy several different personalities and tastes.

A Masterful Office Transformation

Ellen's goal was to transform the uninviting, cold, dark space into a welcoming, warm, and appealing public environment. The new color scheme she chose was bright and fashion-forward, but also worked well with the existing carpet that the client requested be incorporated into the design. One of Ellen's other responsibilities was to make certain that all of the new pieces of furniture were the proper scale for the room size. Specific textiles for the wallcovering, sofa, and chairs were selected for durability and a sleek contemporary sensibility. To address the long continuous run of hall space, Ellen found a striking group of freestanding lighting fixtures. I dare say, the owner of the firm and his associates find it a pleasure these days to go to work.

To see is itself a creative operation,
requiring an effort.   —Henri Matisse

Chapter 9
Art Appreciation

A perk of being in my profession is that everything I do in my spare time—traveling, dining out, or observing nature—all connect to interior decorating. One particular leisure activity that is especially sensitive to my work is cruising art museums. Viewing the impressionistic shadings of a Monet landscape, or the daring mix of patterns by Matisse, or the sensual scale of a single O'Keefe flower, or the mesmerizing color blending of a Rothko is a relaxing and rewarding way to expand my knowledge of color and design.

Using Art to Inspire a Room's Color Scheme

This attraction to art surfaced after I moved to Washington D.C. In lieu of tutoring us on the window displays along Fifth Avenue, Mother turned to guiding us through the varied and imposing collections at The National Gallery of Art, the Smithsonian's Freer Gallery, the Corcoran, or her personal Impressionist pets at the Phillip's. While Mother had her preferences she encouraged us to keep an open mind when looking at the incomparable diversity of art available in Washington. And, unlike most people who rarely notice how museum masterpieces are framed, my mother was keenly aware of the way each painting was paired with an appropriate frame, and for special exhibits even the walls of the gallery are painted to complement the works of art. She never left an exhibit without a catalog, a card, or a poster, a habit I continue to this day.

Jim is now my reliable museum buddy, but our Dec Den friends who join us every two years for Grand Destination trips have accompanied us on jaunts through the Louvre in Paris, the Victoria & Albert in London, and most recently the Hermitage in St. Petersburg. As I was wrapping up this book, a group of us went on a Baltic cruise that took us to some of the most outstanding museums in the world, including the Van Gogh in Amsterdam and the Hermitage in St. Petersburg.

The Hermitage in St. Petersburg.

A sample of Jim's African animal art featuring the giraffe that was the inspiration for my choice of fabric.

My husband capturing a giraffe on canvas that began his lifelong pleasure of painting as a pastime.

The view of our fireplace with Jim's giraffe propped for the photograph.

Back in 1970 on a weekend trip to Bedford Springs in Pennsylvania I lent my restless husband a wooden box full of oil paints and brushes. Seeing his natural ability at bringing a giraffe to life on a canvas, I put away my own painterly ambitions and made him a permanent present of my art supplies. Since that time Jim's art has become a prominent decorative element in our home, but the largest collection of his work hangs in the library.

Our library décor is a bit more Jim-oriented than Carol, but I find the room's African theme equally as appealing as I do my husband. This intimate long and narrow space is home to the artifacts that Jim collected on safaris in Kenya, Mozambique, and Somalia. The faux bois walls are covered with the elephants, zebras, and lions he subsequently painted after his first attempt with a paintbrush. Some years ago leafing through an issue of *British House & Garden* I came across a picture of a chintz designed in 1931, but still in production. The name "Souvenir D'Afrique" and the giraffe motif were enough for me to choose it for the fabric for our library. You can read the story of my custom made-in-Scotland window treatments in chapter 7 on "Designing Windows."

A Unique Display of Fabric Art

Lynne Lawson's long-time client presented her with the supreme challenge of turning an average-sized, architecturally deficient living room into the most spectacular of all the rooms in her house. Zeroing on the plain wall behind the sofa and making it the focal point was Lynne Lawson's solution.

The rich neutral textures of the upholstered pieces and subtle eggplant color of asymmetric turban swags and drapery panels provide a sublime background for Lynne's scintillating wall of art for which she installed twin seamless mirrors adorned with fluted molding on either side of the sofa and added the wall of art in the middle. To satisfy her client's request for something totally unique and dramatic for over the sofa, the decorator devised nine boxes covered in different-colored silk fabric.

Reflections of a World Traveler

Learning what kind of art appeals to a client reveals more about personal taste than almost any other discovery. One avid fine art collector and world traveler sought a room designed around his "Golden Eagle" lithograph by renowned artist Charles Frace that he had purchased many years earlier. In creating a comfortable gathering place for entertaining guests, the decorator took her lead from the earthy blues and browns of the subject matter.

This room is in the basement of the client's home; and while there are two double windows, they are under a deck, making the space somewhat dark. One requirement was seating for six to eight people. Another was that the colors follow those in the artwork, yet maintain a masculine and relaxed ambiance without being too heavy.

Serving as the room's color roadmap, the selection of a paisley fabric in brown and blue for the two lounge chairs picked up the tones in the lithograph, which is now prominently displayed over the mantle. A solid blue texture covers the sofa with polished brass nail heads detailing the shape of the arms and base. In keeping with the masculine theme and to provide extra comfort, the decorator placed a tweed chair-and-a-half and an ottoman by the fireplace. Stationary coin gold drapery panels maximized the window space and light from the outdoors. Neutral-hued floors and walls also help brighten this lower level space.

Divine Design

When the decorator began this project, the client had recently acquired a piece of art at a fundraising auction for her favorite charity. The painting of Madonna and Child has become her prized possession. She loves it for its beauty and rich color, as well as the spiritual message it holds for her personally.

Initially, the client hoped to find a satisfactory spot to hang the painting in her family room, but there simply was not a wall that seemed to do it justice. So, what began as a simple project of hanging a picture ended up being a complete room makeover.

Taking her cue from the Madonna and Child canvas, the decorator devised a refined but lively family room. The basically cream and soft sage color scheme is highlighted with rich reds; rouge in the arched alcoves, raspberry for the Parsons chair, and ruby for the star-shaped ottoman. The delicate curves of the furniture emulate those found in the painting, which happens to fit so perfectly into the existing brick-framed space over the mantle it can only be attributed to divine providence. To soften the hard wood floors the decorator designed a rug of durable sage wool Berber banded in the same black and red floral as the accent pillows. Simple tab top drapery panels hung just beyond the window and door frames, allow natural light to flow into the room.

A Wall of Mixed Media

Adding to the charm of this guest bedroom is a grouping of sophisticated art displayed on the wall behind the twin beds. The selection of black-and-gold picture frames emulates the finish of the painted beds, and helps bring harmony to the arrangement of large vertical portrait sketches, small vintage landscapes, and medium oval mirrors.

Cathi Lloyd's inspiration for the textiles she chose to update the ebony custom built-ins in her client's bedroom were influenced by the intense colors of their abstract oil painting. The silk fabrics for the bed, cornice, and bench are a combination of iridescent gold and hot pink. The box cornice is accented with 28 hot pink buttons that mimic the block pattern of the bed cover. Hot pink also outlines the clean lines of the bench. Cathi always includes a monogram pillow in her master bedroom designs. This one combines initials from both husband and wife.

Imagine this impressively scaled living room, with its 22 foot ceiling, without its brilliant abstract art. In decorating her client's space **Patrice Hawkins** introduced lively geometric designs, but kept to a more reserved color palette. She balanced the rectangles of the folding screen with circle motifs on the chairs and sectional sofa. Contemporary lighting and coffee table add to the Art Moderne atmosphere Patrice created for her client.

Displaying Prized Possessions

One aspiration of a well-traveled professional couple when they hired decorator **Rose Burcheri** to revive their living room décor was to ask her to find a way to display the large and rare white wedding kimono they had purchased years earlier. In doing so, Rose also addressed the issue of the vacant two-story wall behind the sofa. With a Bordeaux satin fabric and a Plexiglas shadow box, she designed a museum quality exhibit to show off this valuable work of art. The awe-inspiring 88 inch by 64 inch display grabs all your attention as you walk into the foyer and look into the living room.

For her own living room, Chris chose an understated elegant style.

Ways of Making a Serene Haven of Your Home

Elegant is defined in *Webster's Dictionary* as "dignified richness and grace; tastefully luxurious." By the time many of our clients, including our own interior decorators, get down to transforming their homes, this is the type of environment to which they aspire.

However, achieving simple refined elegance–whether in dress or design–is not as easy it looks. Let me show you by example the way some decorators achieved quiet elegance in their clients' homes and their own.

Simplicity is the ultimate sophistication.

— Leonard da Vinci

Chapter 10

Evoking Quiet Elegance

Meet the Decorator

For the two decades I have known **Chris Sapienza**, she has been busy raising a family, running a successful decorating business, and as an Interiors by Decorating Den Regional Director managing a large group of franchise owners. Most recently Chris has directed some of her time and talent towards streamlining the rooms of her own residence. The serene, sophisticated results mirror the quiet elegance of the lady herself.

The Decorator's Living Room

Often baby grand pianos are for show, but not in the Sapienza household. Chris, a classically trained pianist, has passed down her love of music to her children. The long narrow living room is used for recitals, visits with family and friends, and hosting business meetings. With a neutral palette and contrasting dark wood, she did an admirable job of maximizing the seating requirements needed for each of these functions. Natural fabrics enhance the spacious feeling presented by the cane back sectional seating. The tone-on-tone cover of the settee reinforces the circle and square motif repeated throughout the room.

Instead of weighing down one end of the space with art, Chris highlighted the wall behind the piano with a decorative grid. A striking over-scaled pharmacy lamp illuminates the piano and helps underscore the focal point. Castors were an efficient solution to moving small tables around for easy access near the various seating arrangements. An understated sisal rug grounds the room and provides sound softening texture. Chris's use of shutters at the windows follows the architectural molding detail and eliminates the need for a busy window treatment.

Regional director and decorator extraordinaire Chris Sapienza.

Chris's Dining Room

In the dining room Chris Sapienza retained her furniture, but developed a decorating scheme to blend with the adjoining rooms. Adding three feet to her ten by ten foot dining room allowed for recessed storage cabinets and drawers to accommodate china and linens. Since all of the surfaces of the room are smooth, she reupholstered the chairs with a textured neutral fabric; and to supply a whisper of pattern and color she added a soft blue, taupe, and white floral Tibetan rug. The black-and-white photographs found at a local art festival and a simple pedestal sculpture add dashes of panache to the room's quiet mood.

Chris's Master Bedroom

One of the first rooms Chris revamped was her master bedroom. There she layered the imposing wood bed with spa blue and soft taupe linens, and a scrumptious mohair throw. By matching the softly patterned carpet to the taupe wallcovering, she blurred the definition of the room's edges. Chris salvaged an old desk and slipcovered it in a silk ticking stripe, which she topped with a heavy one inch slab of glass turning it into a useful dressing table. For architectural interest she added plantation shutters and crown molding which draw the eye upward, giving the impression of higher than eight foot ceilings. Chris says, "Sleek though it may be, it is highly personalized with accessories."

A Modern Classic

The decorating of this dining room was doubly important since it is the first room seen as you enter the home of **Nancy Barrett's** clients. Following the refined tone set by the living room, previously designed by Nancy, are the combination of warm neutrals and dark wood and upholstery. The "X" design of the table and elongated sloping curve of the chairs are classic shapes, but they also reference current fashion. A glass top for the table was an ideal choice for opening up a relatively small space. In response to her client's request, Nancy established a focal point over the sideboard to feature their paper sculpture wall hanging. She highlighted the art further with a pair of buffet lamps adorned with gracefully wrapped shades.

A European Flavored Kitchen

When it came to remodeling her own kitchen, Luisa Maringola was after a casually elegant European look for the space that would be the heart of her home. The decorating journey began with the selection of old-fashioned subway tiles and new cabinets with raised panel doors painted a warm white. Luisa warmed up the kitchen with a large island stained a rich brown. The warm and cool tones of the granite tie everything together.

When needed, the new country table can extend to easily seat ten people. For comfort and color, pads were added to the rush seats of the chairs; and to dress up the window and door, Luisa hung a beautiful floral and bird print. Light fixtures with Old World charm add sparkle and a final European accent.

Making a Major Difference

Looking at these next two decorating projects for different clients it appears that **Connie Thompson** is a master at turning the dreariest of rooms into places of extreme beauty.

In the first situation her clients were searching for ways to make their living space appear less somber than it did with their current furnishings. They wanted a formal adult entertaining area and also a quiet space where they could enjoy their time alone together. Their living room had the additional challenge of being entirely open to the foyer, which made the overall design and furniture placement a predicament these homeowners had not been able to resolve on their own.

Enter Connie Thompson into their lives and their living room became as she described it, "subtly sublime." Introducing a lighter palette was the way she addressed the most pressing

A once dreary living room converted into a serene oasis.

problem. Next, by grouping a screen, floor lamp, and plant at one end of the neutral sofa Connie was visually able to separate the living room from the foyer. To break up the long expanse of windows, the old wood blinds were replaced with striped silk panels over sheers. A high aperitif table holds the accoutrements for after-dinner drinks.

Built-in bookcases were designed to define cozy niches for the furniture, and provide space for displaying family photos. When they are alone, Connie's clients enjoy reading or playing a game of chess while lounging in their comfortable transitional chairs. Connie's idea of monograms on the ample brown pillows offers a trendy fashion accent to her clean, classic revision of this once dowdy space.

Before and after the decorator worked her magic of turning this master bedroom into a restful retreat.

Another extreme makeover Connie did was a bedroom for clients who were experiencing the empty nest syndrome. The husband had recently retired from a stressful job that included prolonged business trips. They were looking for an oasis to retreat to and restore their spirit. Connie described her client's taste as, "leaning towards modern with 'one foot' in the traditional style." Looking through fabrics gave her the idea to use the egg shape/oval pattern, which represents renewal and rebirth, and was meaningful to the wife since she embraces the restorative powers of yoga and meditation.

Using neutrals in cream, brown, and green adds to the peaceful feeling her clients envisioned. Keeping accessories to a minimum assured this sensibility of a calm, serene space. It was important to both designer and clients to select "green" materials wherever possible. The bed sheets are bamboo, the paint is low VOC, and one of the tables is made from recycled wood. The majority of the fabrics and furniture were made in the U.S.A., therefore reducing the environmental impact of shipping. Connie explained, "I took my time to make sure each piece we selected kept the proper balance between modern and traditional, and had relevance to the theme of the room."

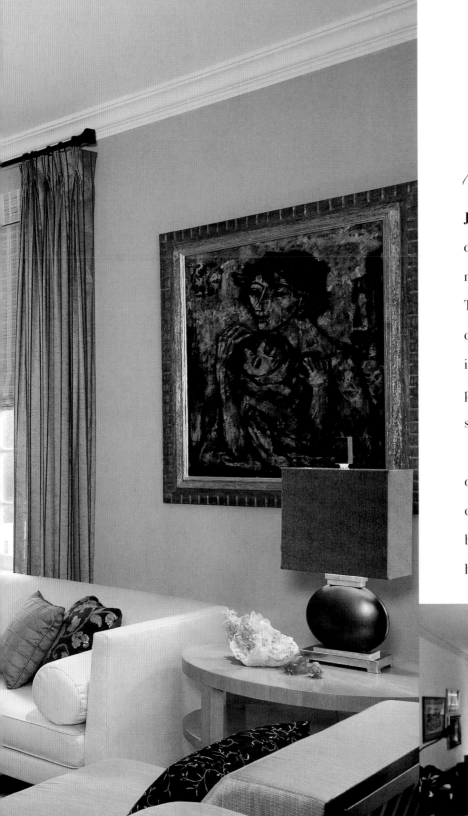

Makeover for a Sophisticated Lady

Jane Speroff's client wanted her out-dated family room to be comfortable and inviting, yet sleek and modern—in other words, more like the successful well-traveled woman she is today. The brick chimney did not match the client's goal, but she was concerned about the time and expense to remove it and replace it with stone. Jane's masterful solution was a Weathered Stone product that completely transformed the chimney and the room's style at a fraction of the cost or work of real stone.

Contemporary furniture and accessories, and tailored drapery panels over woven wood shades cultivated a more client-appropriate atmosphere, and with a neutral palette and black accents, Jane also created a flattering backdrop for the homeowners' collection of original artwork.

Before

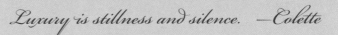
Luxury is stillness and silence. —Colette

Chapter 11

Personal Getaways for Women at Home

Designing Spaces to Restore Body and Soul

Ladies, log off the computer, turn off the TV, silence the cell phone, and retreat to a quiet zone in your home. Whether it is a distraction-free place for meditating, reading, writing, napping, or soaking in a tub—you deserve a pleasant sanctuary where you can go to restore your body and soul. If you are like me, and the late decorator Dorothy Draper, you might try taking advantage of the quiet uninterrupted early morning hours, propped up in bed against a batch of pillows, sipping coffee, and making plans for the day ahead.

Morning Rentrée

Since my *coup de foudre* with our house thirty-two years ago, I have been on a personal mission to make the decorating of the master bedroom live up to its potential. Architecturally it's a gem: luxurious dimensions, original French doors and windows, high ceilings, and a wood-burning fireplace. Decorating-wise I feel obligated to enhance all of these givens.

Waking up in my rustic canopy bed surrounded by my things and soothing blue-greens puts me in a good frame of mind for rejoicing in the day.

I cherish my early morning *rentrée* rituals in the cozy nest I have created within my rustic four-poster dove-embellished canopy bed. From my perch, there are unobstructed views of the fireplace, a built-in bookcase cabinet, my handsome secretary, and a bench under the windows where I enjoy the changing view of the trees in their seasonal dress. The soothing colors of sea and sky were inspired by a long-ago-beach-vacation purchase—the Berthe Morisot print seen on the wall beside my bed.

Other nods to my fondness for French style are the "made-in-China" faithful copy of a Louis XV Savonnerie needlepoint rug, a framed silk scarf of a coastal scene of Nice by Raoul Dufy, and an antique brass-and-pewter chandelier from Brittany.

What I see from my bed... left: a lovely Country French secretary, the fireplace area, and built-in bookcases, below: my view beyond the romantic window setting.

A memento-studded folding screen and vanity table that I enjoy daily.

The only thing missing from my room these days is my beloved dog Bradley.

Taking advantage of the silence and solitude that prefaces the sounds of traffic on our busy lane, I adhere to the advice offered in this chapter's opening sentence. Many of my most creative ideas have been conceived in this fertile environment. The essentials are my coffee, journal, calendar, pens, pads, newspaper, and the latest shelter magazines.

Another personal spot in my bedroom is the skirted vanity table, which I have personalized with a memento-studded lattice-folding screen. It was intended as a temporary fix, but I have grown attached to it and find it impossible to remove a single item without banishing a beloved reminiscence. These days the only thing missing from getting my day off to a great start is the appearance of a black Lab to nudge the side of my bed announcing it is time for me to get up.

The professional touch of the decorators was definitely what turned a neglected space into a charming room devoted to letter writing and journal keeping. A painted chest that fits in the room's small alcove addresses the lady's storage needs.

Correspondence Quarters

I remember seeing this room after IDD decorators from Maryland and Northern Virginia had transformed a tiny eight foot by ten foot space into "Correspondence Quarters" for a National Symphony Show House. The setting they created, while designed for an imaginary lady, would be appropriate for any real woman who preferred to keep in touch with her family and friends the old-fashioned way, by handwriting personal letters. The light painted octagonal table, a lovely alternative to a standard desk, is outfitted with all of the necessary writing accoutrements for penning notes, or perhaps jotting down thoughts in a journal. A pair of comfortable upholstered armchairs would make the room an ideal setting for a tête-à-tête with a girlfriend.

The decorators did not let the meager room size or the below-average ceiling height stop them from creating an exquisite place for the lady of the manor. Both the gorgeous coral tone-on-tone striped paper on the wall and the reflective faux finish on the ceiling helped give the space the appearance of a taller room, and placing the furniture in the center of the room actually allowed for more open floor space, making the room feel larger. And to keep the elegantly draped décor from appearing too stuffy, the decorators added a custom white shag rug.

A Room to Reflect, Relax and Renew

Nature sets the color palette for the restful retreat, labeled "Tranquility Base," that was created by **Sharon Binkerd**, **Myriam Payne**, and **Jennifer Erstein** for an American Red Cross Show House. Lush shades of green in leaf, olive, grass, and lime combined with deep plum produce a restful harmonious feeling. Comfortable furnishings, including a chaise lounge and contemporary sofa, are ideal for relaxing and unwinding. Anchoring this seating area is an unusual area rug and Asian-inspired cocktail table. Slider doors are covered with the wider, newer version of verticals. A wall of silk hides unattractive architectural features and provides a soft backdrop for the photographic art behind the sofa.

Green is more than the color scheme of this multi-purpose room. The decorators were very conscious of choosing eco-friendly products such as water-based paint, natural cork flooring, silk drapery, and sustainable wood furniture. Other earth elements include driftwood nesting tables and a floor lamp with a unique papyrus shade. Finishing off the "Tranquility Base" are the relaxing sounds of music and a tabletop water fountain.

*Inset: Gracing the opposite wall above a
beautiful carved console hangs a piece of
fine photography.*

Left: The deep shade of indigo sets the stage for a restful room dedicated to meditating and designed by Lisa Landry.

Meditation Room

The most important part of **Lisa Landry's** client's master bedroom suite (described in chapter 14) is her meditation room (far left). Since her client meditates every day for one to two hours, it had to be comfortable as well as restful and calming. Also significant was the placement of the tables and shelves, which function as altars. Lisa chose a deep indigo shade for the walls, accented with ebony trim. She added a delicate crystal chandelier that can be dimmed to the client's comfort level. The floor cushion was designed in a size and shape to fit her client's body when in the meditation pose; and for total privacy during her sessions in the room she can close the crimson embroidered draperies.

Prayerful Retreat

To create a sense of privacy for a woman who wanted an intimate sitting room for her morning devotional time, **Alisa Lankenau** and **Heidi Sowatsky** draped the six foot wide doorway shown here with shirred fabric panels made out of reversible fabric edged in blanket fringe. The walls beyond were painted a warm gold and the windows were covered in faux silk. A small writing table, reupholstered Parsons chairs, a favorite rocker, a Queen Anne loveseat, bookcases, and a contemporary light fixture round out the furnishings that go into making this a peaceful retreat for solitary reflection or meeting with the client's Bible study group.

Decorator **Nancy Lucas** *helped her client choose all of the items that went into making her bathroom a tropical paradise. Paint and Italian ceramic tiles are the color of a pink sandy beach, and the border subtly suggests rolling waves. The "whirlpool bath alcove" framed by two columns, features a wallpapered backdrop of horizontal stripes and the homeowner's print that inspired the room's theme. The spa blue drapery panel reminiscent of Caribbean waters conceals a stash of towels and bath essentials. Real and faux plants grouped with candles add to the soothing retreat that Nancy's client loves to escape to at the end of a long day at the office.*

The idea behind this bathroom makeover was to restore it to its turn of the nineteenth century charm. And that is exactly what **Gloria Rinaldi** *helped her client do. Here she repeated the green and blue colors from the bedroom on the walls and even the exterior glazing of this claw foot tub. Privacy is insured with an operable striped Roman shade detailed with black and white polka dot banding and beading. With the light streaming in, the client enjoys slipping a little further back in time when she slips into her vintage bathtub.*

Time Out Soaking in the Tub

In keeping with the master bedroom that **Joyce Means** decorated for her client (See chapter 4), the walls of this adjoining bathroom are quartz-stone textured and faux painted in warm tones of burgundy, green and gold, which complements the new tiling on the floor and walls. The unique curvature of the stunning hammered-copper tub is perfectly situated in front of the ceiling-to-floor windows. Accessories around the tub include a large floor-standing vase filled with silk magnolias, artwork, and shelves decorated with greenery, pottery and birdcages. Joyce installed motorized cellular shades that stack up tightly leaving the view open for her client to watch birds as they come up and perch on the custom-made bronzed "tree-branch" as she is bathing in her gorgeous tub.

The room where I spend my days writing.

Selecting the Right Desk Makes Work a Pleasure

My early obsession with having a private working space of my own was given a boost the summer I turned sixteen. When my mother called long distance asking what kind of a birthday present I would like her to bring back from Peru, I admitted that I had already found what I wanted in a local furniture store. It was a desk, a piece of furniture that precipitated a lifelong attachment to secretaries, writing tables, and the like.

What an adventure I had scouring the town for my first desk. My bedroom was small, but I knew I did not want one that was too petite. The top had to have enough space so I could comfortably spread out my homework, and there had to be drawers to store the usual teenage paraphernalia. I took great care in making my final selection along with a curlicue-arm chair that supplied the necessary contrast to the linear features of the secretary/desk.

The piece I chose was small enough not to crowd out the bed and other belongings, but large enough to take care of my needs. Its simple lines provided me with the classic design I had in mind, and the drawers and desk area made it functional as well. When the slant top was open, it revealed secret letter compartments, niches for books, and ample space to spread out my school papers. I was fond of the idea that I could raise the top and hide my personal things under lock and key.

For the past thirty years a treasured reproduction Regence period desk has been the centerpiece of my private work sanctuary. It used to serve as the place for preparing model home presentation boards, and handling all of the paperwork that went with running my own business. But when I switched to writing books on a word processor, I pulled out the middle pencil drawer, layered it with a piece of wood, and created a place for the keyboard. As with all of the rooms in my house, my writing room is a work-in-progress.

The walls remain upholstered in "Partner's Legacy," the black-and-white toile I designed in honor of one of my devoted Labs. My inspiration rack, pinned to the wall over the fabric, is profusely layered with images I cannot seem to part with; scenes of New York, Paris, and black Labrador retrievers, quotes from the likes of Frank Lloyd Wright, Ernest Hemingway, and Albert Einstein, and treasured photos with family, friends, and dogs.

I recently relocated the file cabinet behind my desk to the hall and replaced it with a wood and iron étagère to house my growing collection of decorating books and magazines. It also holds the Dream Room reference binders that I use on a daily basis closer at hand. My new best piece of furniture is a mid-century modern Eames ribbed black

Chapter 12

Everyone Needs a Great Desk

leather and curved cast aluminum swivel chair, the epitome of sleek functional design, and one of the images on a series of 42-cent postage stamps featuring the designs of Charles and Ray Eames. This classic American icon and the contemporary étagère energize the Country French ambiance of my writing sanctuary.

When it comes to helping clients decorate their workspaces at home nobody has more experience than IDD interior decorators. They are equipped to design offices for clients who run businesses from home, or decorate a space for an individual in need of a private area for personal writing, blogging, or scrap booking.

Some of our decorators maintain outside offices, but most find it convenient to work from design studios set up in their own homes.

42-cent postage stamps featuring the designs of Charles and Ray Eames.

An Interior Decorator's Studio

Decorators are notorious for neglecting the decorating of their own homes, using the excuse that they are too busy creating beauty for clients. When it came time for **Cathi Lloyd** to decorate for herself, she decided to make her design studio not only a pleasant place to run her business, but a luxurious space like the ones she provided her clients.

Cathi's choice of a lively, harlequin, Swarovski crystal embellished wallpaper in black and tan certainly goes a long way towards offsetting the tedium of handling all of the paperwork associated with her business. An exquisite treatment of black taffeta textured with swirls of organza ribbon dresses her window, while a black credenza and zebra covered chairs energize Cathi's full-time business office.

Wine Room and Home Office

Donald Tatera transformed the irritating view of clutter his client saw every night as she entered her home through the garage into a space devoted to a home office/wine bar decorated in the Art Deco style. Now she is greeted by a room painted a luscious pinot noir and a small-scaled kidney-shaped writing table with a unique zebra striped stone top. Paper and books no longer useful were eliminated, while still valued items are stored in the file cabinets behind the desk. Batiste pleated shades address the matters of privacy and glare from the sun. Along with the large wine poster and boxy-shaded lamp, the decorator's choice of a bold abstract pattern on sleek chairs makes for multiple fashion statements.

On the opposite side of the room—fulfilling the client's request for a place to display her wine collection and bar accessories—is a built-in wet bar and wine rack. Donald's idea of a mirror under the rack visually expands the space. The new décor allows his client's entertaining and work to easily overlap without the room feeling crowded.

Scrap Booking

These days a favorite pastime is scrap booking. Decorator **Sharon Binkerd** was asked to transform a downstairs guest room into a study for a lady who wanted a bright and feminine space for reading, letter writing, working on her photo albums, and scrap booking. The renovation began with the decorator's selection of a sunny toile fabric in buttery yellow and Wedgwood blue. Plain walls were given a tea stained effect, and then embellished with the names and birth dates of the client's children and her favorite poem, "You are a Marvel" by Pablo Casals.

Wedgwood blue velvet covers the reading chair, ottoman, and desk chair. Nesting tables are the perfect resting place for a cup of coffee and a lamp. The armoire, on the left, stores albums, children's books, and scrap booking supplies. With a distressed-and-crackle finish, the decorator made the utilitarian file cabinet fit in with the new soft décor. Office essentials are hidden behind a table skirt that matches the drapery panels. Sharon attended to all of the details, making it a pleasure for her client to relax and work in a charming place of her own.

Inset: On the Louis XV style desk, adding a charming touch, but also providing excellent task lighting, is the client's favorite bunny lamp.

Lisa placed a bench in front of the desk so Gussy, the Boston terrier, can keep her mistress company while she is engaged in paperwork.

A Home Office Beauty

Just off the front entry of the new Italian villa inspired home of **Lisa Landry's** client is a large room with a built-in bay and custom bookshelves that was designated as the wife's home office. The couple wanted to play up the European feel of the room, and along with a touch of femininity, have a design that would balance efficiency and organization with beauty and drama.

The process began with the choice of a unique, kidney bean-shaped desk, finished in caviar black and burnished with aged gold embellishments. From the front it appears to be an elegant piece of furniture, but from the back it is a workhorse of a desk, complete with file drawers and pullout work surfaces.

By mirroring the entire wall between the bookshelves, Lisa visually expanded the space and bounced light around the room. In addition the decorator took a framed mirror that had sentimental value to her client and mounted it on top of the wall of mirror–the kind of surprise that Lisa loves to incorporate in every single room she decorates.

A cozy chaise in the bay area makes an ideal spot for the client to read and relax. Framing the bay ornate embellished draperies hung from a black fluted wood pole with a center architectural crest help to make the space feel like a beautifully appointed room, not simply a home office. The delighted client told Lisa, "My beautiful new surroundings somehow make the mundane tasks of bills and paperwork so much more enjoyable."

Pretty as a Peacock

Julie Bass labeled the room she decorated for a Christmas Show House, the Gentleman's Library. She took her inspiration for the color palette and overall design of the space from a silk turquoise-and-gold paisley fabric, which is reminiscent of a smoking jacket or a handsome necktie. A textured peacock-colored faux suede envelopes the room and complements the panels of silk that sweep across the contrasting stationary drapery.

Trompe l'oeil library paper disguises the wall of utility closets and creates the illusion of book-lined bookcases. Taking center stage is a distinctive campaign desk with a tooled leather inlaid top. Julie added sleek armchairs in black leather with gold nail head accents and a sumptuously thick white flokati rug.

Chapter 13

Fostering Tradition

Rooms with Timeless Appeal that Never Go Out of Style

For the past three decades while attending the International Home Furnishings Market in High Point, North Carolina, I have witnessed manufacturers' bi-yearly attempts to introduce new product lines of furniture and accessories that will grab buyers' attention and promote sales. Trade publication editors struggle to find new trends to write about. Only the best ideas take hold and evolve over time into something more permanent. Others simply last a season and disappear. But, it is gracious, comfortable, easy-to-live-with traditional furnishings, gently tweaked to mesh with current expectations that never seem to go out of style.

One gracious corner of the easy-to-live in traditionally furnished bedroom designed by Becky Shearn.

Meet the Decorator

No one does traditional style with more aplomb than longtime franchisee, and IDD Regional Director, **Rebecca Shearn**. A few years ago after Becky and I had spent the day touring the showrooms at the High Point market, she shared with me her plans for a very large project she had designed for her clients. Because of the Dream Room Contest I had always been aware of her decorating ability, but that night I was in awe of Becky's talent for choosing and coordinating products and her extreme proficiency and in-depth organizational skills. Her notebooks recorded every aspect of this monumental project, with detailed record keeping of every important element for each room in her clients' very large house.

Jim and I with Rebecca Shearn and her husband and regional partner Dan in front of The Plaza Hotel introducing a new van concept in 1997. A few years later we revamped our trademark and logo to its current image.

A Room with Timeless Appeal that Never Goes Out of Style

Last year as part of another one of her whole house projects **Rebecca Shearn** decorated a bedroom for a professional couple, parents of a five year old and newborn twins, who as all mothers and fathers would attest to, needed a calming, adult retreat to recharge their batteries.

Working around her client's oriental rug and their passion for red, Becky found a lovely fabric called "Maharajah's Carpet" that was used for the duvet and the drapery and introduced blue into the scheme.

Becky paid special attention to accenting the drapery, pillows, and duvet. For a lighter look during the summer, the duvet can be reversed to an ivory and blue toile, which has been repeated on the shams and roman shades. The China blue tone-on-tone stripe wallpaper sets off the warm cognac finish of the modern classic furniture. Becky's clients are delighted to have a bedroom that makes them feel like they are escaping to an English country inn—or flying off on their own magic carpet.

... the professional touch

One of the advantages of hiring an interior decorator is the attention they give to the details that elevate a room above the ordinary.

Left: Trims, piping, and buttons detail the pillows and duvet.

Right: Becky treated the drapery panels to double piping and covered buttons utilizing fabric from the bed skirt.

Black & White, Always in Style

A black-and-white color scheme works equally well for those who prefer to play it safe and those who want to take a chance. It suits formal moods, as well as casual, and it looks smart with either classic or contemporary furnishings. At the moment it happens to be at the height of fashion, both in apparel as well as decorating, but the longevity of a black-and-white scheme is endless. From the cover of this book, you know it was the color combination I chose to surround myself with in my office.

Changes in taste prompted interior decorator **Judith Slaughter** to inject some new life into her own dining room. While Judith had tired of the room's busy color scheme and patterns, she still liked her traditional furniture and many of her accessories. Contributing to the updated look are a sophisticated black-and-white toile for the walls, and a coordinating fabric for the drapery panels. She had the wainscoting and trim freshly painted white and the ceiling a soft golden ivory. The pattern of the new black area rug

Black, white, and cream smartened up this traditional bedroom designed by Diana Apgar.

picks up the golden tones of the ceiling and her favorite artwork. Judith revived the seats of her graceful Queen Anne chairs in a black figured fabric. Crisp white china, candlesticks, and shell tureen complete the charming renaissance.

Cluttered and no longer displaying the colors and style that resonated with the personality of **Diana Apgar's** clients, she was given the mission of converting their bedroom into a blissful place for sleeping and reading. The decorator's answer to a request for little color was a smart but surprisingly comfortable combination of black, white, and cream for fabrics and floor coverings.

Walls were painted warm and restful "Irish Linen." All of the furniture, including the impressive king-size panel style bed has been finished in antique black. A lovely print was chosen for the tailored duvet cover and also used for the drapery panels, while a solid cream fabric with black cording covers a club chair and ottoman. Diana satisfied her clients' requests, and then some.

A recliner and a petite chair and ottoman meet his-and-her requirements.

Relaxed Traditional Design

After a couple years of using the living room on a very limited basis, **Jane Speroff's** clients wanted to turn this long and narrow space into a serene retreat for adults. The changes began with painting the walls a dark green and replacing the carpet with oak hardwood floors. Capitalizing on the long endwall, Jane placed a long bank of mahogany bookcases to hold the clients many books and personal accessories. A recliner and a petite chair and ottoman, each near direct task lighting, meet the his-and-her requirements for comfort. There is also a loveseat covered in a collage of pattern and solid textures. Softening the floor is a large chocolate brown wool and silk blend area rug. Cherry occasional tables round out the comfortable traditional appearance of this adult haven.

Mixing Tropical with Traditional

To grace the multiple windows and doorway, and the grand mahogany planters bed, decorator **Diana Apgar** picked a white cotton sateen fabric sprayed with flowers and birds, in lush tropical limes and corals. Instead of paint, she chose a subtle striped wallpaper in shades of green, which became a pleasant backdrop for the window treatment. Complementing the more formal floral print, Diana chose a delightful bold green-and-white check for the dust ruffle and pillows. A nice touch was the introduction of black, especially as the wool rug's background color for the large display of orchids. White shutters are in keeping with the sophisticated tropical atmosphere; but on the practical side, they are easy to adjust for sunlight and privacy.

The bathroom décor follows the colors and patterns of the master bedroom. Diana duplicated the bedroom's light and sunny décor. Walls were covered in the matching paper to the bedroom's floral and bird print. Underneath the black patterned rugs is an eco-friendly, durable bamboo floor. Waking up in their delightful master suite is a beautiful way for Diana and her husband to start the day.

Classic Red and Gold
Color Schemes, Updated

The gold and vermillion **Adrian Halperin** and **Ellen Bryant** selected for the draperies and furnishings complement their clients' cherished display cabinet, original artwork, and desire for an elegant living room. Long panels of plaid silk with attached swags frame the windows and carry the color up the golden walls. Serving as the room's cornerstone and providing the rich formality the clients were looking for is a deeply tufted, curved-back sofa covered in a soft gold, small wale corduroy, which helps to keep it from appearing too large in the small open space. A pair of open armed chairs, and a bergère upholstered in contrasting red-and-gold fabrics provide additional seating. Along with new accent tables, all of these elements came together to create the inviting traditional setting the clients preferred.

Barbara Tabak's young clients wanted to update the dining room of the husband's boyhood home to reflect their love of traditional style and the color red. The room was barely 10 feet 8 inches by 13 feet 7 inches. Bold red wallpaper provided instant drama. Barbara followed with a deep faux painted design for the ceiling. Placing open back chairs around a round glass top table created the illusion of space.

Gold tassel-trimmed, embroidered drapery panels and gracefully swagged valances contribute to the room's overall charm. Finishing touches include a grouping of art over the sideboard, an area rug, wall sconces, and a chandelier embellished with a ceiling medallion.

Refined Elegance

Except for keeping some of her antiques, this homeowner longed for a complete makeover for her living room. In addition, since this would be the client's first experience with custom drapery, she wanted something very special. The starting point of transformation was decorator **Marina Collela's** choice of a fashionable palette of soft greens and mellow golds. Next came the selection of furniture for the two separate seating areas. In the one, Marina positioned two elegantly shaped sofas and a pair of matching bookcases, holding family photos and accessories, flanking the fireplace.

On the other side of the room in front of the window, Marina created an intimate conversational grouping around a cocktail table. At the windows, sumptuous textured sage silk panels with attached swags and jabots hang over Austrian shades. "More than I had ever hoped for," was the client's response to her gorgeous custom window treatments and gracious new living environment.

Decorated for a Twenty-first Century Princess

Traditionally styled bedrooms decorated to appeal to young princesses never go out of style. For their four-year-old daughter's bedroom, **Alisa Lankenau** and **Heidi Sowatsky's** clients wanted simple elegance and classic design ... a look and feeling that would be consistent with the rest of their home.

The project got underway with the decorators' choice of pieces from a line of charming children's furniture. Mirrors on the armoire doors and dressing table help to visually open up the 12 foot by 12 foot room. To take advantage of the room's height, Alisa and Heidi installed a crown of drapery above and behind the bed in pink velvet lined with the same plaid as the quilt.

A big-girl chair placed in the corner accommodates both the mother and daughter when it is time to enjoy reading together, and the petite footstool lets the child climb up all by herself. At the window the decorators combined smocked sheers and white eyelet drapery backed with an opaque green fabric that helps keep the light from waking the princess in the morning. To anchor the colors, furniture, and traditional feeling, they added a braided rug as a final touch.

*The decorators created a cozy corner for
mother-and-daughter reading times.*

"Furnishings play a vital role in setting the mood and atmosphere for everyday living," and that "... a woman's home is an extension of herself."
—Bob Mackie

Creating Luxurious Atmospheres

If you believe that glamour is reserved solely for the rich and famous, think again. Or as a busy mother/working woman you cannot picture yourself surrounded with luxurious furnishings, all the pictures in this chapter will show you otherwise. Our decorators have the resources for all the necessary elements that conjure up glamour–shimmering metallics, crystal beads, sumptuous silks, sparkling mirrors, luxurious accents, and more. Each of these dazzling rooms reflects the way decorators satiated their clients' desires for a touch of glamour in their lives.

The Glamorous Bob Mackie

Bob Mackie–a name synonymous with designing glamorous gowns for the likes of Cher, Anne Margaret, Tina Turner, and Carol Burnett–has turned his talent to fashions for the home. Bob Mackie's belief that "it is every woman's dream to be noticed and appreciated for her glamour and elegance" motivates his divine designs for fashions and furnishings.

Bob Mackie at the International Home Furnishings Market in High Point, N.C. showing Carol one of his latest lamp designs. The entire lines of Mackie designed furniture, lighting and rugs are all available through IDD interior decorators.

No one is more glamorous than the handsome, fun-loving, self-effacing Mackie who demonstrates his magnetism on his frequent appearances on QVC. I witnessed this firsthand when Bob was a speaker at an IDD conference. He entertained us decorators with some wonderful stories at a luncheon honoring our DDCD members (decorators who have passed our Certified Decorator test), and at the Dream Room Awards Ceremony where he presented the Decorator of The Year Award. I was not sure our celebrity guest would want to sit through this lengthy awards ceremony, but he did. I asked Bob if he minded if one of our decorators, dressed in a version of his famous Scarlett O'Hara drapery and rod costume for Carol Burnett, could introduce him, and he was delighted.

Earlier he had indicated that he would not give a talk, but after his introduction by Miss Scarlett, Bob Mackie stepped up to the podium and lavishly praised the talent of the interior decorators whose work he had been watching on the screen for the last two hours. He told the audience how moved he was by the genuine warmth and excitement the decorators displayed for their buddies when the winners were announced. We were equally touched by his generous spirit.

Meet the Decorator

There is a certain interior decorator in our company who for me epitomizes the beautiful no-nonsense women of Dec Den who easily merge their natural design ability and business acumen with IDD's support system. I remember meeting **Lisa Landry** shortly after she joined Decorating Den. A bunch of us were at a summer training session in Western Canada. I was impressed that she had come all the way from Dallas, Texas to take advantage of one of Dec Den's advanced education programs.

A few years later when she was a participant on a success panel, I was even more in awe as I listened to Lisa revealing to the next generation of IDD decorators the secrets behind her fast growing business. Since then at our conferences, Lisa teaches one of our most popular business workshops. As for her decorating skills, it was in reviewing her entries in the Dream Room Contest that I was first alerted to her stunning makeovers and the way each room had a touch of Lisa's signature style . . . glamour.

For over a decade Lisa has been managing and mentoring decorators who assist her in taking care of a long roster of delighted clients. One such client commented, "I feel honored to have such a beautiful bedroom." Lisa decorated the room she is referring to with a Taj Mahal theme.

Taj Mahal Inspired Master Bedroom

This oversized master suite is divided into three zones: the main sleeping area, the bay window zone, and the meditation room. The latter is described in chapter eleven. Lisa Landry's starting point on this project was the custom-made upholstered headboard in a Taj Mahal inspired shape. Furthering the opulent look, she combined crimson silk bedding with metallic gold sheer drapery trimmed with crystal beads. Lisa selected new furniture and accessories for her world traveling client that suggest pieces collected over time from her travels.

Lisa Landry receiving IDD's top award (left) and teaching a business workshop at conference.

Inset: In the bay area of this large master bedroom there is an elegant reproduction French daybed with lots of cozy pillows and a super-soft throw. Bronze silk draperies frame the windows, adding a sense of luxury to the pampering zone. Lisa was pleased to report that there is no wasted space in this extra large room. In fact, the client claims, "I use all three zones daily."

The decorator's selection of glamorous
furnishings impacted this small living room.
Below: The classic silhouette of the Klismos
chair is always in fashion.

Suited to Black Tie Entertaining

Decorator **Sheryl McLean** did not let the small size of the living room nor low hung windows keep her from satisfying her clients' request for a glamorous décor with sleek city sophistication. Her social young clients asked for a space that would feel as right for guests gathering in their home for cocktails before a black tie affair, as it would have for that debonair Hollywood film couple, Nick and Nora Charles.

A warm neutral palette was the first step in making the room feel more spacious, and Sheryl's infusion of blue supplied interest without being overpowering. Playing to the room's best feature, nine foot ceilings, Sheryl visually expanded the window's proportions with drapery panels flowing from underneath deep box-pleated valances.

The openness of the backless double-arm white chaise, glass and metal tables, pair of classic Klismos style chairs, and a cocktail table with a graceful X base contribute to the alluring new look of this room, while also perpetuating the appearance of a grander space. Accents like a faux mink throw, sparkling mirror, and orbit table lamp put the final luxurious stamps on the décor. Sheryl's expertise in selecting the appropriate colors, scale, and textures for the new furnishings transformed a lackluster living room into an elegant place for entertaining in the grand style preferred by her discerning clients.

The Allure of Glamour   193

Luxurious Retreats

A Sumptuous Retreat

Luxurious drapery fabric and an elegant chaise evoke true glamour in this bedroom retreat. It was hard to decide where in this book to place the sumptuous bedroom corner designed by **Sharon Binkerd.** The chapters on windows or women's retreats would have been appropriate, but I deemed the best place was here in "The Allure of Glamour." I recall when I first saw this Dream Room vignette thinking what an elegant oasis Sharon had created for a busy mother of three little ones, and oh how envious her friends must be when they see the languorous recamier, angled in front of gorgeous silk draped windows.

Ciao Bella

Who wouldn't feel beautiful going to bed and waking up in this *bella* room? The decorator made the bed even more gorgeous by covering it with luxurious cream-and-bronze quilted silk bedding and overstuffed red velvet shams edged with glass beaded *passementrie*. They solved the problem of an unsightly view out the door with a custom sized trompe l'oeil mural, which creates the illusion of stepping through the iron gates onto a balcony to view the garden. Lamps, a painted chest, a chandelier, and an oversized mirror, all in the Italianate style, add to the room's romantic ambiance.

A gorgeous iron bed, dressed in luxurious fabrics, sets the stage for a romantic bedroom.

Silver tones and touches changed a dreary
living room into a place of beauty.

...the professional touch

Women have a concept of glamour, and decorators have the resources
for satisfying their visions with sumptuous finishes, fabrics, and
furnishings.

Above: By papering the ceiling as well as the walls with this shimmering silver antique tile-like paper, decorator Shelley Rodner doubled its effectiveness and added dazzling sparkle to an ordinary, bland bathroom. Simple dotted sheers hanging from a sliver of silver rod with crystal finials, the gorgeous mirror, crystal chandelier, lovely sconces, and mirror-covered vanity also play important roles in glamorizing this small bathroom. A few black accents add dramatic contrast.

Livable Glamour

These next three fabulous transformations remind me of those magical magazine makeovers where ordinary women are turned into glamour gals. Soft palettes, simple but stunning window treatments, and shimmering silver elements contribute to their fabulous new looks.

With a softer color scheme and a different furniture arrangement, decorator **Lynn Lawson** revitalized her own gloomy living room. Instead of the predictable pieces of living room furniture, she created a pleasant conversational grouping solely with chairs in a variety of styles and fabrics that have been centered around a 30 inch high glass-top pedestal table. Shimmering spa blue and sparkling silver provide the "bling." French pleated silk drapery panels, adorned with tassels, and hung on silver-toned rods, complement the silver wall and ceiling covering and chest.

New window treatments and furnishings enhance the scale and add drama to the former blah dining room (top left). To give this dining room the glamour and drama that the homeowners desired, **Myriam Payne** used creams accented by silver and gold, contrasted against the dark, high-gloss of the furniture. The sumptuous wallpaper contains metal powder and fibers that give texture and reflect the light of the modern clear glass and silver chandelier and the crystal and gold buffet lamps. High-back side chairs were covered in micro suede, which is soft to the eye and comfortable to sit on. The valance and draperies were designed to maintain the graceful curve of the arched windows.

The Allure of Glamour 197

Chapter 15

Perpetuating a
Key West Attitude

Key West Images: My Story

People often proclaim how grand it would be to keep the Christmas spirit all year long. My dream, after residing every February in Key West, is to maintain the island's laidback attitude for the next eleven months. Jim and I came here on our honeymoon forty years ago, and now we cannot imagine a winter without Key West. We are convinced that every day spent in this tropical paradise is adding years to our lives. The moment I begin driving the last 100 miles to Key West,

I put a moratorium on worry. Like the Christmas spirit, however, preserving an easygoing disposition all year long is hard to do.

When I am back home and feel stressed out, I try to picture myself walking along a stretch of Smathers Beach, or ambling down Duval Street to purchase a tropical trinket from Fast Buck Freddies, or sipping a margarita while watching a blazing sunset from Mallory Square. For me, nothing symbolizes the "getting away from it all" resort feeling as the overall ambiance of Key West. Here are the ways some IDD decorators perpetuated that relaxed feeling for their clients.

*Left: The style is transitional and the mood
is "the livin' is easy."*
*Inset: After being reupholstered in spa blue,
the clients' old wicker wingback chairs mesh
beautifully with the updated furniture.*

Indoor/Outdoor Living

In Florida it is hard to discriminate between indoor and outdoor living since they both flow together so easily. A prime example is this two-story riverfront residence that was originally intended as a vacation home. The challenge of this project for decorator **Judy Underwood** was to incorporate some of the major pieces from her clients' former, traditional home into a more refined, transitional home for year-round use as they eased into retirement.

The custom wall unit was retained and the clients' wicker wingback chairs were reupholstered in a new soft spa blue fabric. A glass and iron table sits atop a contemporary wool area rug that was selected to set the palette and complement the colorful artwork. Soft, flowing, fixed drapery panels frame the self-pocketing sliders, which are open to the lanai much of the year.

Comfortable all-weather chairs were selected for the adjacent wrap-around lanai overlooking the pool for frequent casual entertaining. The centerpiece of the sitting area is a five by seven foot cocktail table cut from a 400-year-old oxcart from Asia. New seating with waterproof cushions and designer fabrics provide all-weather entertainment comfort. The concrete patio flooring was painted a lighter color to match the exterior vinyl siding and the living room tile floors so that the interior space flows into the outdoor lanai area.

Enjoying the Outdoors All Four Seasons

Not everyone is aware that outdoor furniture is available from IDD, but we do have a variety of options for good-looking, weather-protected furniture and fabrics. To accommodate her clients' needs, decorator **Cynthia Hammersley** chose teak furniture complemented with woven "faux rattan" accents made of a long-lasting polyurethane product, formulated especially for outdoor use. Teak has a virtually unlimited outdoor life, even when exposed to the elements in all

climates. Using cubicle hardware and grommets, Cynthia also provided her clients with drapery that could close off parts of this patio "room" as needed to eliminate glare on the TV (not shown) and to reduce the heat from the late afternoon sun. The drapery fabric is reversible and highlights both the rust and the gold color palette established with the banquette cushions.

This photograph captures a newly furnished terrace in all its glory at twilight. When decorator **Kathy Machir** built a new terrace as an extension off of her living room, she had some of the same challenges as those of the previous story. Kathy and her husband Jim entertain frequently and needed to establish a setting that would be pleasant both during the day and at night. For the conversational grouping she chose natural teak and in the dining area black wicker, with cushions for both areas in tropical colors and patterns. To block the wind and sun, Kathy installed Sunbrella fabric draperies with a heading of grommets that blend in with the natural surroundings.

Creating A Year-Round Paradise in Your Own Home

Storage benches with removable seat and back cushions were custom fitted inside the gazebo. At night a bamboo cage lighting fixture illuminates the vibrant tangerine voile covered ceiling.

The responsibility of transforming the nondescript, uncomfortable outdoor space at an American Red Cross Show House into an inviting entertainment area was given to the decorating team of **Sharon Binkerd**, **Jennifer Erstein**, and **Myriam Payne**. They came up with a stunning design that called for multiple seating arrangements in shades of cream and melon with the gazebo as the focal point. For the patio, a grouping of chairs was brought together with a canopy of sheers to create a cabana style area. All of the fabrics, lighting, and rug selections are made for all-weather living. Future residents of the house can kick back and enjoy the decorators' carefree modern interpretation of a comfortable outdoor retreat.

The new décor perpetuates a year-round paradise.

A Sunset Palette

Lisa Landry had decorated every room in her clients' home before they decided to tackle their master bedroom. They craved an updated, modern feel, and the "boutique-hotel-in-a-tropical-locale," as Lisa describes the aesthetic that resonated with her clients. To that end Lisa developed a palette of sunset orange, wet sand, and espresso. The starting point was a platform bed with minimalist bedding.

To create a second zone in the room, she added a funky velvet chaise to the bay window area, along with a great reading lamp and convenient table. Draperies in an espresso sheer, alternating with a satin stripe, frame the amazing view of their beautifully landscaped yard. The addition of palms, a tribal art wood-strip mirror, woven sea grass vases enhance the feeling of being on vacation every day.

One final touch was a coordinating dog bed for the clients' beloved Chinese Shar-Pei, Frodo. Lisa designed an oversized cushion, using the same fabric as the bed throw, which slides easily under the platform bed in morning, only to be pulled out each night for Frodo's sleeping comfort. The client's love the fact that it's concealed when not in use.

Creating Carefree Spaces

Warming up the stark white of a porch that her client had enclosed into a sunroom was **Lorraine Brown's** challenge. The decorating also needed to be kid friendly, and be worked around an entertainment center and black leather chair. Lorraine took the chill off of the space with a combination of warm tropical wicker and wood furniture, fabric for the chairs and pillows with a palm tree motif, a lively patterned rug, and on the practical side, a dirt-proof (well almost!) red fabric for the sofa.

Because the space is so long, decorator Lorraine Brown divided it and put a table and four chairs at the far end for eating, doing homework, or working a puzzle. The window treatments bring your eye up and balance the furniture, without sacrificing the light. Lamps and accessories complete the attractive sunroom that has become a year-round hangout for the family.

Key West Rooms in other Zipcodes

The home might be in Maryland, but the colors, pattern, and furniture decorators **Lynne Lawson** and **Lori Doughly** chose for this room suggest that carefree Key West attitude. The wall color makes it a sunny space even on dreary days; and the gold, green, and red scheme appeals to both the husband and wife, who do not always agree on color.

Lynne and Lori created visual interest by mixing florals with stripes, and brown and honey-toned wicker. A large-scale chaise and extra comfortable rocker are angled to accentuate the unusual shape of the room. The rocker has cup holders, a magazine/newspaper rack, and is a favorite for the early morning coffee drinking ritual. The storage cocktail table and tall chest hide away paperbacks, candles, and the kids' homework. Woven wood shades complement the furniture, filter the light, and provide needed privacy.

The client told her decorator **Carolyn Jordan** that she loved being outside and had always envisioned enjoying leisurely times on a "Southern" style porch. That was Carolyn's clue to her selection of comfortable brown-toned wicker and rattan furniture. Some of the cushions are covered in a tropical print on a red ground and others in an aqua stripe for a lively color scheme. There are benches under the round glass-top table that can be pulled out for additional seating. An eating nook is conveniently located near the doors to the mini kitchen and family room. Bordered area rugs separate the space for relaxing and dining. Carolyn helped her client realize what was once only in her dreams.

Tropical patterns and wicker furniture
conjure up a summer attitude no matter
what the season.

Your home is the most important part of your life. Unless it is charming and creative, it remains nothing more than shelter! A gracious atmosphere in your home makes you feel radiant and happy. — Arlene Francis

Not everyone is interested in allocating the time and funds to decorating an entire home all at once. In most situations, doing it one room at a time makes more sense. The challenge is decorating each individual room to suit its particular purpose, without losing sight of the total house. Maintaining the essence of the design concept and color scheme throughout–while capturing the personality and preferences of the client–calls for an enormous amount of skill and expertise; and, something else, what I like to think of as innate talent more associated with music, as in a person who can play "by ear." Added to their training, all good interior decorators have a natural ability to decorate "by eye."

The Pleasure of Working with a Decorator Who Cares

When it comes to scope, style, and specifics each IDD decorator's story is as unique as his or her individual clients. Nevertheless, there is a common thread that continues to surface in the Dream Room Contest write-ups and in my conversations with both decorators and their clients–and that is the "we" factor. Throughout this book I have referred to what the decorator has done to improve her client's rooms, but more often than not our decorators recall their work as a collaborative effort–"we chose," "we decided," "we found."

Bonnie Pressley sitting to the left of longtime client Sarah Byar in her newly revamped kitchen

Meet the Decorator

A perfect example of this "we" relationship is **Bonnie Pressley** and her client Sarah Byar. Bonnie has been decorating Sarah's house, one room at a time, since 1996. When I asked Bonnie to describe her rapport with Sarah, this is what she told me.

Sarah was referred to me by my sister, another client of mine. Our first appointment was typical—sharing ideas and client desires. A week later upon my return visit, Sarah's husband called while I was there with news that he had been diagnosed with liver cancer. Sarah and I proceeded with the dining room and a few small projects. Larry passed away in 2000. Since then we have been working together on almost every room in her home—one room at a time.

Our relationship is one of friendship and mutual respect. Sarah has a vision for her decorating, and I "pull it together." It is always a pleasure to work with Sarah, as she is thoughtful and appreciates my time, opinions, and expertise.

We share the same goal on every project—getting every detail just right. Our design philosophy is simple: We keep a balance between "antique" and "new" product selections to maintain the warmth of "old" and the freshness of "new."

Each design selection—whether it be paint, a piece of furniture, fabric or the smallest of accessories—is carefully and thoughtfully chosen. This results in incredible design satisfaction and pride—for both Sarah and me.

The initial project that launched this longtime relationship was the dining room. It was a modest makeover, but there was something about the way Bonnie interpreted her client's requests that caught my attention and made her Sarah Byar's longtime interior decorator. Several years ago I had the pleasure of meeting Sarah Byar in person when she graciously invited me and Bonnie's local IDD colleagues for lunch and a tour of her home.

The Kitchen — from Contemporary to French Country

The most recent makeover has been Sarah's kitchen. In its day it was serviceable and pleasant enough, but thirty-five years later Sarah's taste had changed to her current love of antique French country and the sterile contemporary laminated style no longer suited her. The footprint of the kitchen and the stained brown concrete floors did not change, but the room was completely gutted. Bonnie advised and helped Sarah with all of the arduous remodeling decisions, beginning with the selection of a distressed "feather down" white finish for the cabinets and the "dill weed" color choice for the walls that led to earthy and textural countertops.

Decorator Bonnie was definitely into the details when it came to the European looking accent tiles, the addition of tiny "diamonds" to the field of off-white tiled backsplash, the divided-light glass sections at the top of the cabinet doors, arched display shelves above the stove and sink areas, a wine rack, and oiled bronze fixtures and hardware. Instead of a typical kitchen island, they found a French dining table, added five inches to the legs and turned it into an ideal workstation. Two Provincial style stools and a pair of chandeliers complete the functional and attractive section of the room.

In the breakfast area Bonnie redesigned the window, allowing side casements to open and increasing the size of the window seat, which also resulted in storage drawers. Very generous down-filled cushions now provide comfortable seating and viewing by both Sarah and her dog Mattie. The windows are adorned with light and airy embroidered linen, installed on a custom wrought iron rod.

Since the room is relatively narrow and the need for a large centered table was not necessary, a small antique breakfast table and chairs found on one of their antiquing expeditions was positioned on one wall opposite a kitchen *vaisslier* or cabinet. Sarah admits that she never expected her kitchen could be *more* wonderful than she had dreamed.

Before

Mattie

217

Sarah's Bedroom— Now Her Own

Sarah's master bedroom went through several incarnations before it became her ultimate softer, fresher, and more feminine private getaway. Earthy colors were replaced with pale pistachio walls with

soft white for the trim and doors. A new pair of French doors opened up the dark right corner of the room. Bonnie explains, "Our theme was botanical and vintage. We used a washed-look linen for the draperies and then softened the exterior light in the day with a semi-sheer Belgium lace Roman shade. A mix of antiques and Sarah's own personal keepsakes make the room her own."

... the professional touch

The "we" factor in the relationship between Sarah and Bonnie so beautifully represents the signature style of Interiors by Decorating Den.

Inset: Before Sarah's bathroom had good bones, but it was time to get rid of the huge spa tub and mountain cabin feel and create a more feminine and attractive room.

Sarah's Bathroom — A Relaxing Feminine Space

Once the necessary construction improvements were attended to, Bonnie had all of the stained oak trim, cabinets, and doors painted a soft white and the walls painted the same light pistachio tone of the bedroom. A free-standing cabinet provides space for storing linens, and a hand-tufted wool area rug softens the hard-surface floor and adds color and pattern to the predominantly white room.

The Client Story

The first thing Sarah Byar told me about Bonnie was that over the years they have become great friends. She related how after their first meeting, when Bonnie arrived with an armful of fabrics, catalogs, and pictures that related to the things they had discussed on the phone, "I realized we would be working together for a long time, decorating each of the rooms in my home. Bonnie has introduced me to color and design ideas I would never have thought about. And, although we've redecorated one room at a time, using different color schemes, Bonnie has made my rooms flow beautifully together."

Jim's painting captues the enduring pleasure of sunsets at Poverty Point.

Happiness is not something we can seek or possess directly for its own sake; but it is the sign and reward of a well-directed activity. The happy man is one who without seeking it directly, inevitably finds joy as a by-product in the continuing process of achieving the fullness of his own possibilities.

—Pierre Teilhard de Chardin

Epilogue

I remember early in our marriage a discussion about the definition of success. My husband and I were sipping Drambuie in front of the fireplace in my new home. "First of all," Jim said, "no one is a success or a failure. It is a process. We are either succeeding or failing."

That night Jim and I shared our views of what succeeding meant to each of us. Naturally, at the top of our lists was the desire for a long and happy marriage. A close second was feeling a sense of accomplishment—me in my design career, Jim with franchising.

Longevity does not guarantee success, but we are coming up on our fortieth year of marriage and the founding of Decorating Den. I have determined that if you are lucky enough to survive the ups and downs, marriages built on mutual love and respect not only live on, they grow deeper. Likewise, businesses founded on sound ideas and principles only continue to improve. Any raised eyebrows and doubtful speculation by others has long been put to rest, and Jim and I are more committed and excited than ever to keep both ventures in a succeeding mode.

As for my readers, I hope the revelations in this book have given you the confidence to call an interior decorator to assist you in transforming your house into the home of your dreams. And for those who after learning that I am an interior decorator respond by saying, "Oh, that's what I always wanted to be," may you be inspired to "do something about it." Most of all, I trust that in applying positive changes to your home and your life, you will find happiness in achieving the fullness of your own possibilities.

What never seems to change is people mispronouncing "Donayre," chuckling at the sound of "Bugg," and referring to our franchsie as "DecoratOR's Den."

Photographer Credits

Aurora Photography, 136-137

Bartholomew, Paul S., 46-47

Beall, Gordon, cover, i, vi, x, xii, xiv, xvi, 38, 50-53, 68-69, 72-75, 90, 92, 150-153, 162

Benson, Zack, 106-109, 203

Burke, Patricia, 160

Ellison, Eddie, Accent Photography, 48, 161

Emberger, Paul, 183

Foulds, D. R., vi, xviii, 44-45, 56-59, 66, 76-77, 86-87, 96-97, 99, 120, 130-131, 144-145, 154-155, 172, 174-177, 180-182, 192-193, 195-197, 208-211

Hahle, Matt, 42-43

Hill, Bob, 60-61, 142, 159, 186-187

Hoachlander, Alice, 62-63

Ingrahm, Jeremy Mason, 104-105

Janis, Bryan, viii, 18, 22-23, 70

Johnson, Scott, 54

Lapeyra, Joseph, 112-113, 156-157, 166-167, 194, 197, 200-201, 204-205

Lilly, David, 202

Marshall, Alec, 148-149, 184-185

Merriman, Dawn, 134, 164

Moist, Michael, 101

Olman, Bradley, 110-111

Olson Photographic LLC, 178-179

Roth, Eric, 26

Ruthkatz, Richard, 102-103

Sanders, Jeff, xx, 30-37, 82-85, 99, 135, 211

Seltzer, Greg, 40, 165

Solomon Associates Inc., 13

Taylor, John, 101

Taylor, Rick, 27

Trigiani, Johnny, 64-65

Umber, John, 128-129

Vaughn, Ken, 78-81, 100, 114-117, 158, 168-169, 190, 206-207, 214-219

Yarwood, Ted, 143, 160

Decorator Credits

Apgar, Diana 177, 180-181

Baker, Dolores 46-47

Barber, Diane 104-105

Barrett, Beverly 66

Barrett, Nancy 142

Bass, Julie 99, 130-131, 170-171, 195

Binkerd, Sharon 156-157, 166-167, 194, 204-205

Brown, Lorraine 208-209

Bryant, Ellen 182

Bugg, Carol Donayre i, vi, x, xii, xiv, 12, 38, 50, 52-53, 74-75, 90, 92, 124-125, 150-153, 162

Burcheri, Rose 136-137

Carroll, Julie 195

Coleman, Karen 118-119

Collela, Marina 184-185

Doughly, Lori 210-211

Elliott, Barbara vi, xviii, 44-45, 82-85, 96-97, 110-111

Erstein, Jennifer 156-157, 204-205

Ervin, Terri 27, 54

Fawcett, Anne 26

Fernandez, Ellen, 120

Giar, Sally xx, 30-31, 33-37

Grier, Jeanne 64-65

Halperin, Adrian 182

Hammersley, Cynthia 202

Hartley, Karen 128-129

Hawkins, Patrice 135

Hill, Gloria 56-59

Jenkins, Victoria 195

Jordan, Carolyn 99, 132-133, 211

Lafferty, Tracy 42-43

Landry, Lisa vii, 78-81, 158, 168-169, 190, 206-207

Lankenau, Alisa 159, 186-187

Lawson, Lynne 126-127, 196, 210-211

Lloyd, Cathi 134, 164

Lucas, Nancy 160

Machir, Kathy 106-109, 203

Maricle, Ali vii, 100

Maringola, Luisa 143

McLean, Sheryl 192-193

Means, Joyce 48, 161

Miller, Kris 101

National Capital Region, 154-155

NOVA Region, 154-155

Owens, Susan 102-103

Payne, Miriam 112-113, 156-157, 197, 204-205

Pinkus, Brenda 101

Pressley, Bonnie 98, 214-219

Price, Suzanne 76-77

Riddiough, Lauren 68-69, 72-73

Rinaldi, Gloria 160

Rodner, Shelley vii, 62-63, 197

Sapienza, Chris 138-141

Shearn, Rebecca vi, 86-87, 172-175

Shivers, Nola 104-105

Slaughter, Judith 27, 176

Smith, Cheryl 101

Smith, Luella 88-89

Smith, Virginia 114-117

Sowatsky, Heidi 60-61, 159, 186-187

Speroff, Jane 148-149, 178-179

Tabak, Barbara 183

Thompson, Connie 144-147

Tatera, Donald 165

Underwood, Judy 200-201

VanderHulst, Tonie 40

Ward-Woods, Jennifer vi, xviii, 44-45, 82-85, 96-97, 110-111,

White, Renee 195